VALLEYVIEW SCHOOL LIBRARY
Denville, New Jersey 07834

# THE
# RHYTHM
# AND
# BLUES
# STORY

ALSO BY GENE BUSNAR

*Careers in Music*
*It's Rock 'N' Roll*
*Superstars of Country Music*
*Superstars of Rock*
*Superstars of Rock 2*

# THE RHYTHM AND BLUES STORY

## GENE BUSNAR

VALLEYVIEW SCHOOL LIBRARY
Denville, New Jersey 07834

JULIAN MESSNER  New York.

Copyright © 1985 by Gene Busnar

All rights reserved
including the right of reproduction
in whole or in part in any form.
Published by Julian Messner,
A Division of Simon & Schuster, Inc.
Simon & Schuster Building
Rockefeller Center
1230 Avenue of the Americas
New York, New York 10020

JULIAN MESSNER and colophon are
trademarks of Simon & Schuster, Inc.

Manufactured in the United States of America

Design by Stanley S. Drate/Folio Graphics Co. Inc.

VALLEYVII                                    BY
    Deoville

10 9 8 7 6 5 4 3 2

**Library of Congress Cataloging in Publication Data**

Busnar, Gene.
    The rhythm and blues story.                    *87211*

    Bibliography: p.
    Includes discographies and index.                   *784.5*
    Summary: Traces the development of rhythm and blues
music, from its origins in African music, blues, and         *BUS*
gospel, through the influences of Motown and soul, to
its effect on current performers such as Bruce
Springsteen and Prince.
    1. Rhythm and blues music—Juvenile literature.
[1. Rhythm and blues music]   I. Title.
ML3521.B      784.5'4      85-13691
ISBN 0-671-42145-X

# CONTENTS

## ACKNOWLEDGEMENTS

I would like to thank Doc Pomus, Bobby Robinson, Arlene Smith, Gary Bonds, Screamin' Jay Hawkins, Junior Walker, and Big Joe Turner for the personal interviews and insights that helped shape this book. Thanks to Carl Skiba and the rest of the staff at *Record World*, Patti Conte of Atlantic Records, Neal Hollander of Banner Talent, Phillip Namanworth, Alan Grubman, and my editors, Suzanne LeVert and Iris Rosoff, for their help.

PICTURE CREDITS: Warner Brothers, 2; Record World, 3, 12, 18, 19, 23, 35, 47, 51, 53, 59, 62, 66, 71, 74, 75, 81, 85, 94, 100, 101, 105, 110, 111, 118, 128, 129, 130, 133, 136, 139, 141, 147, 150, 155, 159, 161 (top), 167, 173, 181, 187, 191, 192, 193, 194, 197, 201, 212; Epic Records, 13; Carl Skiba, 16, 209; Neil Hollander, 33; Terry Mills, 41; Billy Vera, 92; Atlantic Records, 156; Capitol Records, 161 (bottom)

# CHAPTER 1

# RHYTHM AND BLUES

## Where We've Been and Where We're Heading

Popular music has always been a matter of personal taste. The songs that live inside your memory are the ones you grow up with. Generations will always argue with each other about whose music was better.

In the fifties and sixties, parents would tell their kids: "This rock 'n' roll stuff, it all sounds like noise. Give me Tony Bennett, *give me the big bands.*" And now, some members of the Woodstock Generation are saying, "Prince. Well, he's all right, but I'll take Sly and Jimi Hendrix."

Everyone is entitled to his or her own personal taste. But when a handful of scholars, musicians, and devoted listeners started talking about rhythm & blues and rock 'n' roll as art forms in the sixties, many "sophisticated" people became outraged. An essay by author Tom Wolfe in *The Kandy-Kolored Tangerine-*

Prince—drawing from tradition and breaking new ground.

*Flake Streamline Baby* typified the way men and women of culture regarded this "primitive music" and its performers:

> Once it was power that created high style. But now high styles come from low places, from people who have no power, who slink away from it, in fact, who are marginal, who carve out worlds for themselves in the nether depths, in tainted "undergrounds." Rock and roll (comes) out of the netherworld of modern teen-age life, out of what was for years the marginal outcast corner of the world of art. . . .

For those who shared Wolfe's feelings, the worst piece of European classical music had far more value than the ranting and shouting of some illiterate Negro or some young white boy trying to sound black. Things are a bit different now that the rock 'n' roll generation of the fifties and sixties has so much of the money and power in American society. Today, rock superstars move in many of the same circles as Tom Wolfe and his friends, but the breakthroughs have come slowly.

In 1967, the famed conductor Leonard Bernstein admitted that he liked rock 'n' roll—especially the Beatles. Suddenly, rock was in. "If it's good

**Mick Jagger—part of today's cultural power structure.**

enough for Bernstein," people figured, "then it's good enough for me." Nevertheless, almost two decades after rhythm and blues–based music became a recognized art form, far too many of its greatest contributors are still struggling to survive.

Fortunately, there are more and more popular performers who do pay tribute to the unsung musical geniuses and their great traditions. People like Prince, Bruce Springsteen, Peter Wolf, David Bowie, and Cyndi Lauper know where their roots lie. The music that inspired these performers to play and sing are the rhythm and blues styles that took shape in the fifties and sixties. But the music had its beginnings decades—and even centuries—earlier.

Rhythm and blues is rooted in the pain of slavery, in the sweet harmonies of a Baptist congregation, and in the roughness of a bluesman singing in some gutbucket juke joint in the rural south. The pounding dance beat, the searing guitars, the raspy vocal styles, and the wailing saxophone solos that have become rock trademarks are all extensions of earlier rhythm and blues styles.

"Rhythm and blues is music about the pain you have suffered," says singer Screamin' Jay Hawkins. "It's about having a good time, feeling passion, experiencing humiliation. It's about your mother dying, your woman walking off, even a bottle of wine. Rhythm and blues is a slave who picked cotton. It's a black man who ran from a lynch mob. It's something of pain, something of bliss, something of love, something of hate, revenge, or laughter. Whatever the emotion, all great music is based on things you actually experience through living."

## Ushering in the eighties with the last of the great blues shouters

Everyone has his own starting point in rhythm and blues. A young musician in the eighties might have to work his way back from Eric Clapton or Michael Jackson or Bruce or Prince. But remember, all these people were inspired by someone who preceded them. Eric Clapton listened to the bluesmen of Chicago, Memphis, and the Mississippi Delta. Michael Jackson listened to Jackie Wilson and James Brown. Bruce Springsteen listened to Gary Bonds and Bob Dylan. Prince listened to Sly Stone and Jimi Hendrix. When I ask the legendary songwriter Doc Pomus who inspired him, he answers without hesitation, "It was Big Joe Turner."

Big Joe Turner and Doc Pomus.

I'm sitting with Doc in a small New York City club called Tramps on New Year's Eve, 1981. The featured performer is about to take the stage. Big Joe Turner gets up from his table and slowly walks across the room, aided by a pair of crutches. Less than ten seconds after his first number begins, it occurs to me that I'm hearing one of the greatest rhythm and blues/ rock 'n' roll singers of all time. I wonder how many people even know who Big Joe Turner is.

Jerome "Doc" Pomus is the world's most unlikely groupie. In his late fifties and confined to a wheel chair, Doc has been a fixture on the New York rhythm and blues scene for years. A blues singer who turned songwriter in the fifties, Doc has penned hits for Elvis, Ray Charles, B.B. King, the Drifters, and many others. His classic songs include "Youngblood," "Suspicion," and "Save the Last Dance for Me." Though Doc himself is a major contributor to the history of rhythm and blues, he sounds like the world's biggest fan when he talks about his hero:

> Joe has always been my idol. When I was young, I used to stay up all night listening to jazz. One night, I accidentally tuned in to a black station and heard Joe Turner sing. From that moment, my life changed completely. The only thing I wanted to do from then on was sing blues something like Joe Turner.

In the forties, Doc started singing at small blues clubs in Greenwich Village. Soon, he met his idol, and they've been close friends ever since. Over the years, Doc has had his share of success as a songwriter, but Joe hasn't fared as well.

Now it's the eighties, and Doc is helping Joe find

Doc Pomus, when
he was a blues
singer.

work in New York clubs. One day he gets a phone call. Great news! The Blues Brothers had recorded Joe's "Flip, Flop and Fly," and the album is in the top ten. The Blues Brothers, John Belushi and Dan Aykroyd—a couple of good comedians with marginal vocal talents—are making a million dollars off Joe's music. But that's okay; Joe should pick up a bundle in songwriting royalties. "You're going to make a fortune," Doc tells Joe as they eat lunch in Doc's Upper West Side apartment. "What do you mean?" Big Joe Turner asks. "I haven't seen a dime off those old songs in ten years." "That can't be," Doc tells him.

Here's what Doc discovered when he checked out the situation for himself:

> Ten years ago, Joe moved from New Orleans to L.A. Since then, he had never received royalties. So I called up [his publisher] and spoke to the guy in charge of bookkeeping. I said: "Let me ask you a question. How come Joe Turner doesn't get any royalties on his songs?" He said: "We've been sending his royalty checks to New Orleans, he's been cashing them in." I said: "He hasn't received a royalty check in ten years."
>
> Here's what was happening: Joe's ex-wife had been living at his old address and cashing his checks. We found out just in time because his publisher was about to send him a royalty check for $26,000. Joe Turner had been close to poverty for the last few years, and suddenly, he picked up all that money at once. If he didn't just happen to mention that he hadn't been getting any royalties, he would have lost $26,000 on that one check and much more in the future.

Today, most musicians are a little more aware of business. They all have lawyers to take care of such matters. But it never occurred to Joe Turner to call up his publisher to find out what was happening to his checks, or to say, "Hey, I'm changing my address."

"Joe's kind of naive," Doc explains. "It's kind of sad the way so many rhythm and blues singers get ripped off. Joe's been beaten many times, but he doesn't go around sour. When Joe leaves a place, he just forgets about it."

Joe was luckier than many. At least he got *some* of the money he had coming. But what a career Joe Turner could have had if the music industry had more of an interest in exposing his talents instead of always going for the quick buck. It boggles the mind to think of what might have been if greed, racial prejudice, and general ignorance didn't always figure so prominently in the mix.

But later for all that. It's the eighties now and when Big Joe Turner sings, he shakes you out of your seat. Crippled and in his sixties, he still has a voice so powerful that he almost doesn't need a mike to over-power the five-piece backup band. In between sets, I ask Joe what young people in the eighties can find in this music. Joe seems hesitant, but Doc picks up the slack. "I think I can answer for Joe."

> Rhythm and blues is soulful. It comes from deep inside, and it's musical, not hostile. [A lot of punk and heavy metal] is not musical, it's hostile and it's . . . not from deep inside. There's something hateful and cold about that kind of music. But what can be more soulful than the blues?

> Do you realize that when Joe Turner dies, he's the last of the shout-blues singers. When he dies, it is all over, there's not going to be another great shout blues singer left and there aren't many breaking in.

As usual, Doc hits the nail right on the head. Young people still have an opportunity to go out and hear Joe Turner, B.B. King, Ray Charles, Bobby Bland, James Brown, and other great rhythm and blues artists. Ten or twenty years from now, it will be too late to go out and see many of these fantastic performers, so it's essential to seize the opportunity while it's still there.

I remember how close I came to never seeing the great New Orleans piano giant, Professor Longhair.

Almost by accident, I caught him at a club on what turned out to be his final tour before he died in 1980. I knew that he had inspired a long list of my favorites, from Fats Domino to the Band to Dr. John. But the man wasn't a great singer, and his records weren't particularly inspiring. Still, if I hadn't caught Professor Longhair's act when I did, I would have missed seeing the greatest pure rock 'n' roll musician ever to put ten fingers on a keyboard.

Then, a couple of weeks before Muddy Waters died in 1983, I was once again reminded that rhythm and blues performers often don't make it to a ripe old age. A friend tried to convince me to catch that powerful bluesman at a local club. "I've seen Muddy a dozen times," I told him. "I know," my friend warned. "But this might be your last chance." A few weeks later, Muddy Waters died.

I started thinking about all the Rolling Stones fans who had never seen Muddy. How, I wondered, would they really understand where Jagger was coming from? And how could they pass up the chance to see the people who laid the groundwork for today's brightest rock stars?

The Rolling Stones' Keith Richards once candidly expressed surprise that anyone would want to listen to his band's version of a Muddy Waters song when they could just as easily buy the original record. But to many rock listeners, the difference between the Stones and Muddy Waters was not so much one of how well the message was being delivered, but who was delivering the message. The average teenager saw much more of himself in Mick than in Muddy. The result: Jagger and his band became rich and famous, while Waters died in relative obscurity.

For better or worse, audiences often are more concerned with how a performer looks than how he sounds. Young people want to buy records and attend concerts of performers they can relate to. Teenagers in the fifties had an easier time relating to Elvis than to Little Richard, just as their counterparts in the sixties found the Beatles and the Stones more to their liking than the black artists those groups were imitating.

To some extent, the same thing is going on today with reggae and other authentic black musical styles. "No matter how exciting the original music is," says Doc Pomus, "a lot of white kids would rather hear other white kids doing it—even if it's a bad imitation. Somehow, it's just more palatable to them." Recently, though, there have been some important changes for the better.

## A new beginning(?)

Wherever you look today, you see more and more rock artists associating themselves with rhythm and blues. "We Are The World" by U.S.A. for Africa is, among other things, a great example of rock artists paying tribute to their rhythm and blues mentors. Many of today's listeners may not immediately associate people like Hall & Oates, Steve Perry, Huey Lewis, Kenny Loggins, and Billy Joel with rhythm and blues. But their singing on "We Are The World"—as well as on many of their own records—makes it clear that this is where their music is rooted.

The rhythm and blues influence is equally apparent in the music of English rock acts like the Police, Culture Club, Rod Stewart, and Phil Collins. Like

**Tina Turner—on top at last.**

their American counterparts, these musicians borrow freely from rhythm and blues styles like Motown, Philadelphia Soul, Stax-Volt, funk, and Reggae. Rock stars on both sides of the Atlantic are usually quite open about their musical influences, and often encourage their fans to seek out the original sources. Apparently, people are beginning to listen.

As I write this, the three biggest acts in rock are Michael Jackson, Bruce Springsteen, and Prince. Is this a coincidence? Maybe so. But I'd like to think of it as a promising sign that young people are becoming more open in their musical tastes.

Who would have imagined that a black man could become to the eighties what Elvis was to the fifties and the Beatles were to the sixties? Yet that is exactly what Michael Jackson has accomplished. In the wake of the tremendous success of Michael's "Billie Jean" and "Beat It" videos, there are more black faces on MTV and more black voices on rock radio stations than there have been in years. When Michael invites Eddie Van Halen to play a guitar solo on "Beat It," or when he records a duet with Paul McCartney, part of the message to rock fans is this: Racial barriers have no place in music.

Michael Jackson—
the '80s answer
to Elvis and
the Beatles.

In spite of Michael Jackson's enormous influence and undeniable talents, however, his impact on the future of rhythm and blues and the acceptance of other black artists is uncertain. Nobody can really guess what direction he will follow. He may decide to record a duet with Barbra Streisand or Frank Sinatra. Or he may decide to pursue the more rock-oriented direction of "Beat It," or the exciting dance rhythms of "Want to Be Starting Something." The guess here is that he will mix it up for a while in order to satisfy both his own varied tastes and that of a mixed audience, which has come to include virtually all races, ages, and both men and women.

In the long run, Prince may have more of a lasting influence on rhythm and blues than Michael J. Although Prince isn't nearly as good a singer as Michael, he is just as good a performer and probably a better songwriter. What may be more important, though, are Prince's more hard-edged sensibilities. So far, there are no indications that Prince will opt for the middle of the road. He seems to have no plans of working the Las Vegas nightclub circuit and no aspirations of attracting an older, more "sophisticated" audience. As he stated in a rare interview with *Musician*'s Barbara Graustark:

> . . . I have definite viewpoints on a lot of different things: the school system, the way the government's run and things like that. And I'll say them in time . . . But if people don't dig my music, then stay away from it, that's all. It's not for everybody, I don't believe. I do know that there are a lot of people wanting to be themselves out there.

Prince may be thinking about the future of his music, but he leaves no doubt about his roots. In his highly acclaimed film *Purple Rain,* Prince is clearly paying homage to various rhythm and blues influences. His onscreen rival, Morris Day, is a takeoff on James Brown and other soul performers. Prince's own playing and stage movements show that he is a great admirer of both Jimi Hendrix and Sly Stone— the two black performers who were most successful in attracting white audiences in the sixties.

While Prince and his band, the Revolution, are performing in *Purple Rain,* the camera pans to crowds of both white and black kids digging the music of this racially and sexually mixed group. This is the kind of scenario that makes the future of rhythm and blues, and popular music in general, look brighter than it has for some time.

Bruce Springsteen is another superstar who seems to be pointing the way to better things. Though his audience is primarily white, it is clear that many of his musical roots are in soul music and other authentic R&B styles. Writer Chet Flippo recently called Bruce "the hardest-working white man in show business." This was an unveiled reference to the debt Bruce owes to black performers like James Brown for inventing the kind of hard-working, high-energy performance Springsteen has become famous for.

Bruce usually refers to what he does as rock 'n' roll, though I've always felt that he would be just as accurate if he said rhythm and blues. In any case, when he talks about his music and his audience, you can tell that Bruce is unconcerned with making racial or any other kind of political distinctions.

The music Bruce and his E Street Band make is "a human thing," Bruce recently told a *Musician* interviewer. "It doesn't matter what the problems are or

**Bruce Springsteen—"the hardest working white man in show business."**

what the government is like. It bypasses those things. It's heart to heart." Perhaps that is why Bruce ended every concert on one recent tour by shouting, "Let freedom ring."

In the past, rhythm and blues and its performers haven't enjoyed all the benefits of freedom and equality in America. For years, the music industry referred to rhythm and blues as "race music"—music made by black recording artists and tailored for black listeners. But the time has finally come to put prejudice aside and recognize rhythm and blues for what it is, the major underlying force in our best popular music over the past thirty years.

As I see it, rhythm and blues is not just important historically or limited to any one particular race. It's a living, breathing force in today's music. If you forget about skin color and fashion, you'd be hard pressed to find much of a difference in the musical sensibilities of Boy George and Smokey Robinson, Keith Richards and Chuck Berry, Bruce Springsteen and Gary Bonds, Rod Stewart and Tina Turner, the Police and Bob Marley. It would be a mistake to categorize white musicians as rock and black musicians as rhythm and blues when their music is so much alike.

All great music—no matter how it's labeled—comes out of a sense of personal and social struggle. "The hardest wheel," the saying goes, "has been put through the hottest furnace." When today's better rock performers want to make powerful, emotional music, they draw from the deep well of rhythm and blues because they know that stuff is real.

## SELECTED DISCOGRAPHY

### DAVID BOWIE
*David Live at the Tower Philadelphia* . . . . . . . . . . . . . . . . . . . RCA
*Diamond Dogs* . . . . . . . . . . . . . . . . . . . . . . . . . . . . . . . . . . . . . RCA
*Let's Dance* . . . . . . . . . . . . . . . . . . . . . . . . . . . . . . . . . . . . . . . EMI
*Scary Monsters* . . . . . . . . . . . . . . . . . . . . . . . . . . . . . . . . . . . . RCA
*Station to Station* . . . . . . . . . . . . . . . . . . . . . . . . . . . . . . . . . . RCA
*Young Americans* . . . . . . . . . . . . . . . . . . . . . . . . . . . . . . . . . . RCA

### PHIL COLLINS
*Face Value* . . . . . . . . . . . . . . . . . . . . . . . . . . . . . . . . . . . . Atlantic
*Hello, I Must Be Going* . . . . . . . . . . . . . . . . . . . . . . . . . . Atlantic

The Pointer Sisters, Chaka Khan, Hall & Oates, and Billy Joel—just a few of today's stars whose music is grounded in rhythm and blues.

## JOHN COUGAR

American Fool . . . . . . . . . . . . . . . . . . . . . . . . . . . . . . . . . . . . . Riva
Nothing Matters and What If It Did . . . . . . . . . . . . . . . . . . . Riva
Uh-Huh . . . . . . . . . . . . . . . . . . . . . . . . . . . . . . . . . . . . . . . . . Riva

## CULTURE CLUB

Colour by Numbers . . . . . . . . . . . . . . . . . . . . . . . . . . . Virgin/Epic
Kissing to Be Clever . . . . . . . . . . . . . . . . . . . . . . . . . . . . . Virgin
Waking up with the House on Fire . . . . . . . . . . . . . . . . . . Virgin

## HALL AND OATES

Private Eyes . . . . . . . . . . . . . . . . . . . . . . . . . . . . . . . . . . . . . RCA
Rock 'n' Soul . . . . . . . . . . . . . . . . . . . . . . . . . . . . . . . . . . . . RCA
Voices . . . . . . . . . . . . . . . . . . . . . . . . . . . . . . . . . . . . . . . . . . RCA
$H_2O$ . . . . . . . . . . . . . . . . . . . . . . . . . . . . . . . . . . . . . . . . . . . RCA

## MICHAEL JACKSON

Off the Wall . . . . . . . . . . . . . . . . . . . . . . . . . . . . . . . . . . . . . Epic
Thriller . . . . . . . . . . . . . . . . . . . . . . . . . . . . . . . . . . . . . . . . . Epic

## BILLY JOEL

An Innocent Man . . . . . . . . . . . . . . . . . . . . . . . . . . . . . Columbia

## PROFESSOR LONGHAIR

Crawfish Fiesta . . . . . . . . . . . . . . . . . . . . . . . . . . . . . . . Alligator
New Orleans Piano . . . . . . . . . . . . . . . . . . . . . . . . . . . . Atlantic

## THE POLICE

Ghost in the Machine . . . . . . . . . . . . . . . . . . . . . . . . . . . . A&M
Synchronicity . . . . . . . . . . . . . . . . . . . . . . . . . . . . . . . . . . . A&M
Reggatta de Blanc . . . . . . . . . . . . . . . . . . . . . . . . . . . . . . . A&M
Zenyatta Mondatta . . . . . . . . . . . . . . . . . . . . . . . . . . . . . . A&M

## PRINCE

Controversy . . . . . . . . . . . . . . . . . . . . . . . . . . . Warner Brothers
Dirty Mind . . . . . . . . . . . . . . . . . . . . . . . . . . . . Warner Brothers
1999 . . . . . . . . . . . . . . . . . . . . . . . . . . . . . . . . . Warner Brothers
Prince . . . . . . . . . . . . . . . . . . . . . . . . . . . . . . . . Warner Brothers
Purple Rain . . . . . . . . . . . . . . . . . . . . . . . . . . . . Warner Brothers

## BOB SEGER AND THE SILVER BULLET BAND
*Against the Wind*.................................Capitol
*The Distance*...................................Capitol
*Live Bullet*.....................................Capitol
*Night Moves* ...................................Capitol

## THE TIME (featuring Morris Day)
*Ice Cream Castle* ........................ Warner Brothers

## JOE TURNER
*The Best of Joe Turner*...........................Atlantic
*Big Joe Rides Again* .............................Atlantic
*His Greatest Recordings* ..........................Atlantic
*Sings K. C. Jazz* ................................Atlantic

## TINA TURNER
*Acid Queen*................................ United Artists
*The Best of Ike and Tina Turner*.................. Blue Thumb
*Black Man Soul* ................................Pompeii
*Come Together* ........................... United Artists
*Don't Play Me Cheap* ................................SUE
*Festival of Live Performances* ........................ Kent
*Greatest Hits*............................. United Artists
*Nutbush City Limits*......................... United Artists
*Private Dancer* ................................Capitol
*River Deep Mountain High* .........................A&M
*Sixteen Great Performances* .........................ABC
*World of Ike and Tina Turner* ................. United Artists

## PETER WOLF
*Lights Out* .........................................EMI

# CHAPTER 2

# RHYTHM AND BLUES ROOTS

*Sometimes I feel like a motherless child,*
*Sometimes I feel like a motherless child,*
*Sometimes I feel like a motherless child,*
*A long way from home, Lord,*
*A long way from home.*

—*Afro-American Spiritual*

It's very easy to turn on the radio and hear the latest Michael Jackson, Prince, Culture Club, Tina Turner, or Hall and Oates record. It's even easier, somehow, to turn on MTV and watch these performers do their thing. But as we've seen, today's best musicians and performers did not develop their styles in a vacuum. Space limitations prevent a full exploration of every musical style and every single rhythm and blues performer who had an impact on what we hear today. Still, this story can't really be told without going back decades and even centuries.

All of the rhythm and blues, jazz, and rock we hear now are products of black people's experiences in white America. Unlike most of the European immigrants who came to America to find better conditions,

blacks were brought here by force. This dramatic difference in their circumstances is an important key to understanding how black music evolved.

Beginning in the late fifteenth century, black Africans were forcibly removed from their tribes, and chained in the holds of ships by mercenaries. Those who survived the cruel conditions of their long voyage were taken ashore in a strange land and sold to the highest bidder.

Slaves were the absolute property of their masters. They were allowed no possessions and no freedom of choice or movement. Slaves were not permitted to practice their African religions or speak in their native tongues. The masters felt that the suppression of all African customs would reduce the slaves' temptation to escape. Many of them also believed that blacks were better off as slaves in a white Christian society than living as free men in Africa. This attitude gave slave owners a sense of righteousness as well as a cheap source of labor. Around the time of the Civil War, Alexander Stephens, an official of the Confederacy, justified the practice of slavery this way:

> [The foundations of slavery] are laid. Its cornerstone rests upon the great truth that the Negro is not equal to the white man; that slavery—subordination to the superior race—is his natural and normal condition. . . . It is best, not only for the superior, but for the inferior race, that it should be so. It is, indeed, in conformity with the ordinance of the Creator.

Naturally, the slaves didn't see the situation in quite the same way. To the contrary, they recognized that in order to maintain their dignity as human beings, they would have to keep their African traditions alive and pass them on to future generations.

The life of a slave was a painful one, but the music that grew out of these sad conditions laid the seeds for rhythm and blues, jazz, and rock 'n' roll. The chants and rhythms, which were important parts of every African's life, were passed on from generation to generation of slaves. In spite of the masters' attempts to repress African singing and drumming, the spirit of this music survived.

In Africa, music was the pulse of everyday life. All events, however large or small, were represented by a different song or drum beat. Since there was no written language, African tribes used music to document historical events and pass on information. Important happenings, such as a boy's initiation into manhood, marriage, or death, were marked by elaborate rituals. These religious ceremonies were all accompanied by the proper song.

As in Africa, transplanted black Americans used music to express their deepest, most intense emotions. From the beginning, black American folk music was rich with the raw sounds and feelings that stemmed from the pains of slavery.

Since slaves spent most of their waking time engaged in hard labor, they developed songs to help lighten their load and keep up the pace. This tradition also harked back to Africa, where singing had long been a natural part of group work. Black Americans, like their African counterparts, sang their work songs in a *call-and-response* pattern.

When a leader sang a line in the fields, the chorus either repeated his call, added to it, or sang a contrasting line. Long after the slaves were freed in 1865, groups of workers, in the fields, on ships, or on cattle ranges, kept the traditions of black work songs alive.

Perhaps the closest current music to the singing of field slaves is the chanting of prisoners on chain gangs in the rural South. One of the better-known prison work songs is called "Take This Hammer":

*Take this hammer—huh!—carry it to the captain—huh!*
*Take this hammer—huh!—carry it to the captain—huh!*
*Take this hammer—huh!—carry it to the captain—huh!*
*Tell him I'm gone—huh!—tell him I'm gone—huh!*

*If he asks you—huh!—was I runnin'—huh!*
*If he asks you—huh!—was I runnin'—huh!*
*If he asks you—huh!—was I runnin'—huh!*
*Tell him Ise flyin'—huh!—tell him Ise flyin'—huh!*

In this song, the leader calls out each line, holding the last word as long as he can in order to give his comrades a little rest. As the convicts swing their hammers in time to the song, they answer *huh* in a grunting chorus. By doing so, the prisoners express their feelings about the harsh prison life and the cruel guards they call "captain." This call-and-response style of singing also helps the chained convicts to move as one.

A good singing leader is vitally important to how well the rest of the group do their work. On some work gangs, especially skillful song leaders are excused from the actual work. In his book *Negro Folk Music,* Harold Courlander explains the leader's role in call-and-response singing:

The singing leader is as essential to the work gang as the . . . preacher is in the church. He must have the feel of the work that is being done, an understanding of the men with whom he is working, and the capacity to evoke both music and [movement]. As in the dance, music and [movement] are inseparably joined. Although the prime objective of the gang song is not entertainment, it nevertheless must be more than melody, words, and timing; the song that captures the imagination of the workers, that engages them, will get the work done by keeping the men in a working spirit. For members of work gangs, either on the railroads, or in prison battalions, many of the songs they hear are part of an old and familiar repertoire. A good singing leader senses what kind of song is needed at a given time, and how to sing it. Frequently, he has a talent for improvisation or new creation. A good many work songs were heard for the first time only moments after the events on which they comment took place. Some action of the boss or "captain," some overheard conversation, a passing woman, a quarrel, or anything else may be turned into a song if the leader can grasp it and distill it into a singing statement. Sometimes a leader improvises on a theme that has personal meaning to him, but in such terms that it can have personal meaning for the other men in the group.

As with work songs, black religious singing was also often conducted in a call-and-response style, with the preacher serving as leader. Black religious sects were patterned after Baptist, Methodist, and other white Protestant churches, but the sermons had more in common with African religious ceremonies than with the sermon that a white preacher might be conducting just a few short miles down the road.

While slaves were forbidden to practice African religions, they were encouraged to convert to Christianity. This they did in large numbers. Many blacks found abandoning their native religion a painful emotional experience. Still, Christianity did offer the slaves a way to express their hardships and their hopes for a better life after death.

Blacks brought much of the strong beat and frantic emotions of African rituals to their practice of Christianity. In some of the more spirited black churches, congregations of slaves would stomp their feet on the bare floors, achieving an effect close to African drumming. After hours of repetition, some of the worshipers became "possessed" and shouted ecstatically while flinging themselves to their knees. This closely resembled the trance state of "spirit possession" in some of the old African religions.

Another, less frantic type of religious song, the spiritual, reached its peak in the mid-nineteenth century. Spirituals represent a more sophisticated, less raw kind of black religious singing. Songs like "Go Down, Moses" and "Swing Low, Sweet Chariot" used the events and language of the Bible to express the plight of Negro slaves. Here again, a call-and-response pattern is utilized, with the preacher as leader and the congregation as the responsive chorus:

> LEADER: *Swing low, sweet chariot,*
> RESPONSE: *Comin' for to carry me home.*
> LEADER: *Swing low, sweet chariot,*
> RESPONSE: *Comin' for to carry me home.*
> LEADER: *I looked over Jordan and what did I see?*
> RESPONSE: *Comin' for to carry me home.*
> LEADER: *A band of angels comin' after me.*
> RESPONSE: *Comin' for to carry me home.*

Many black religious songs were simply variations or reinterpretations of white hymns. Yet even in recent years, great black religious singers like Mahalia Jackson, Clara Ward, and Aretha Franklin still find simple, traditional hymns of British origin like "Amazing Grace" relevant to contemporary life:

> *Amazing Grace, how sweet the sound*
> *That saved a wretch like me.*
> *I once was lost, but now am found*
> *Was blind, but now I see.*

Religious hymns are only one type of English/ Scottish folk song that black Americans continue to utilize in their music. Like many African chants, English/Scottish folk music is centered around only a few basic notes. There was something immediately familiar in the simple melodies of these songs that made them comfortable for the early slaves to sing. As the slaves adapted European notions of melody and harmony, they added their own rhythms and vocal inflections.

Slave children quite naturally picked up the songs of their white playmates. At the same time, the white children became exposed to black inflection. In some cases, a gifted black youngster would learn to play an instrument by eavesdropping on the music lessons of one of his master's children. As slaves were sold to new plantations, they exchanged songs with their new companions.

This social and musical give-and-take between slaves and their masters continued through several hundred years of slavery. By the time emancipation came in 1865, the mixture of black and white folk music had evolved into some vital new song forms.

## SELECTED DISCOGRAPHY

*Afro-American Spirituals, Worksongs and Ballads.* . Library of Congress
*Black American History in Ballad, Song and Prose.* . . . . . . . . . Folkways
*Negro Prison Camp Worksongs* . . . . . . . . . . . . . . . . . . . . . . . Folkways
*Roots of Black Music in America* . . . . . . . . . . . . . . . . . . . . . Folkways
*Songs of the American Negro Slaves* . . . . . . . . . . . . . . . . . . . Folkways

# CHAPTER 3

# THE BLUES

*The blues ain't nothin' but a lowdown, achin' heart's disease*

—Robert Johnson

Slavery legally ended at the end of the Civil War, but the newly freed blacks did not have an easy life. Because many blacks, practically speaking, had nowhere else to go, they continued to work as sharecroppers on the same plantations on which they had been slaves. Others left to seek work elsewhere. For better or for worse, black people were now on their own. This newfound sense of isolation and displacement was the basis of blues singing.

Most of the early blues singers experienced lives of rootless wandering through the South. While slavery had totally restricted the black man's freedom, emancipation forced many black people to roam from one migrant labor to another. Thus, many blues lyrics are concerned with poverty, wandering, loneliness, and fear of the law. As Arnold Shaw notes in *The World of Soul:*

> The Negro made music from his earliest days on this continent. But it was communal music: to pray to, to lighten labor, occasionally to dance to. . . . But the singer had to see himself as an individual and personalize the group's experience before the work song [and other kinds of group singing] could emerge as a blues.

Obviously, this could not . . . [happen] until some time after the Emancipation Proclamation. The slave had to be separated from the land to which he had been feudally attached and given awesome mobility. The food and shelter provided on the plantation had to be taken away and the "freed" man given the freedom to starve and scramble for necessities. The new man had to discover the world of penitentiaries and chain gangs and romantic sex and a bottle of gin before he began to sing:

*"When a woman takes de blues*
*She tucks her head and cries.*
*But when a man catches the blues*
*He catches a freight train and rides."*

The earliest blues forms utilized the voice as the featured instrument. Blues was used to express feelings and thoughts, and for dancing and entertainment. But originally, as Shaw notes, the blues was mostly "the itinerant music of men traveling from farm to farm, lumber camp to lumber camp, town to town, and, unquestionably, sweetheart to sweetheart."

The first blues singers wandered through the South, accompanying themselves with their guitars as they sang about their lives, loves, and hardships. The early blues singers used a musical form in their songs known as a *twelve-bar structure.* This structure came from European music, but the vocal and rhythmic techniques of the blues were African in origin.

Most conventional blues songs use a *three-line form* within the twelve-bar musical structure. The first line makes the statement, which is repeated by the second line; the third line concludes the thought. This traditional twelve-bar blues and three-line structure can still be heard in many current rhythm and blues and rock records. One example of this style is

the Robert Johnson classic "Love in Vain," which was
later recorded by the Rolling Stones:

> *Well I followed her to the station with a suitcase in my hand,*
> *Well I followed her to the station with a suitcase in my hand,*
> *Well it's hard to tell, it's hard to tell when all your love's in vain.*

Another important feature of blues singing—
one that stems directly from African music—is the
bending or slurring of notes. This effect is accomplished by singing or playing a note so that it falls in
between the conventional tones of a scale. These
notes, which are usually slight alterations of the third,
fifth, and seventh steps of the conventional major
scale, are usually called "blue notes." These tones cannot be written in musical notation and run against the
traditional European notions of correct singing.

As the blues evolved, they were used more and
more as dance music. Wandering blues singers like
Blind Lemon Jefferson knew they would starve if
they didn't fill their tin cups with change. Somehow,
on payday or at harvest time, there was always a blues
singer around, stomping his feet to make sure the
crowd would hear the beat of the music. Once the
crowd got happy and started to dance, they would be
more inclined to throw some coins into the cup.

The blues had its first golden era in the 1920s
and 1930s. A number of great blues performers
emerged at that time, most of them only a generation
or two removed from slavery. The majority of these
singers came from Mississippi or Texas. Some of the
most important blues artists of this period include
Blind Lemon Jefferson, Big Bill Broonzy, Son House,
John Lee Hooker, and Robert Johnson.

Chuck Berry—his sound was clean enough for white radio stations.

Of all these great blues performers, Robert Johnson had the strongest influence on today's rhythm and blues and rock. Born in Mississippi around 1910, Johnson displayed genius in his singing, guitar playing, and song writing. The music he made with his voice and guitar, accompanied by his stomping feet, sounds like a complete band. If you listen past the scratchy recording quality, you can almost hear the steady bass line, the tinkling piano fills, and the

VALLEYVIEW SCHOOL LIBRARY
Denville, New Jersey 07834

pounding drum of a four-piece electric blues band. In fact, the next generation of blues singers simply hired sidemen to play the lines that Johnson was doing by himself.

Robert Johnson recorded some twenty-six sides for the Vocallion label in a makeshift studio that was set up in a Dallas hotel room. As is often the case with great works of art, Johnson's music and lyrics have taken on a meaning that seems to go beyond the events in his life and the world in which he lived.

Though the exact biographical details are rather sketchy, we do know that Robert Johnson was a poor black country boy who wandered around the South playing in roadhouses and juke joints. His experiences resembled those of many black people in the rural South. In one of his better-known songs, "Crossroads," he described the terror of being stranded in a racist town after dark:

> *I went down to the crossroads, fell down on my knees.*
> *I went down to the crossroads, fell down on my knees.*
> *Ask the Lord above for mercy, say boy, if you please.*
>
> *Standing at the crossroads, I tried to flag a ride.*
> *Standing at the crossroads, I tried to flag a ride.*
> *But nobody seemed to know me, everybody passed me by.*

Although this song refers to a particular time and place, the words seemed just as meaningful when Eric Clapton, a white Englishman, sang them on Cream's *Wheels of Fire* album in 1969. Johnson's words and music, reinterpreted by this three-piece electric band, sounded just as vital as ever. But Clapton, like many of the musicians who idolized Johnson, didn't only copy his notes. He also tried to under-

Eric Clapton—
evoking the spirit
of Robert Johnson.

stand the forces that drove Johnson to such creative
heights.

Robert Johnson seemed to be haunted by evil
spirits and evil women. According to legend, Johnson
was killed by one of these women. He often spoke in
his songs of finding the right kind of woman but he
always seemed to wind up with one who gave him
grief:

*I got a kind hearted woman, do most anything in this world*
*    for me.*
*I got a kind hearted woman, do most anything in this world*
*    for me.*
*But these evil hearted women, man, they will not let me be.*

—"Kind Hearted Woman Blues"

As a commercially recorded singer, Johnson made a lot of money for his time and place. Sometimes, the women that he was attracted to used him, then left when the money ran out. He describes such an experience in "Walking Blues":

*I woke up this morning, feeling around for my shoes.*
*I woke up this morning, feeling around for my shoes.*
*But you know about it, I've got these old walking blues.*
*Lord I feel like blowing my old lonesome horn,*
*Got up this morning to find it was gone*
*I got up this morning, all I had was gone.*

The vague pieces of Johnson's life, as revealed by his songs and a few scattered pieces of biographical information, tell the story of a certain type of man— one pursued by spirits and the need to roam. Having the blues is one thing, but living the blues is another issue completely. The factors that caused the early bluesmen to leave their homes and wander were a strong feeling of restlessness and the desire to break away from a poor and deprived life-style.

Perhaps these are similar to the reasons why, a generation later, Little Richard wrote "Tutti Frutti" while working as a dishwasher; why a young Jerry Lee Lewis slipped into black clubs to hear the blues; and why Elvis Presley sang the way he did in his early years. All three of these men, like Robert Johnson, seemed to have been conducting their own personal struggles with the devil: Little Richard with his constant switching between preaching and popular singing; Jerry Lee Lewis with his many wives and problems with drugs and alcohol; and Elvis, the shy country boy corrupted by too much fame and fortune.

One way or another, these artists were all wrestling with forces seemingly beyond their control. Perhaps, like Robert Johnson, all great blues singers are driven by a feeling that they are somehow being chased—be it by a woman, the law, or an imagined evil spirit. This sense of eternal restlessness is captured in Robert Johnson's classic, "Hellhound on My Trail":

> *I got to keep moving, I got to keep moving,*
> *Blues falling down like hail, blues falling down like hail.*
> *I can't keep no money, hellhound on my trail,*
> *Hellhound on my trail, hellhound on my trail.*

Even though he seemed to be desperately running away from something, Johnson still found a moment in the middle of this song to smile:

> *If today was Christmas Eve, if today was Christmas Eve*
> *And tomorrow was Christmas Day,*
> *If today was Christmas Eve*
> *And tomorrow was Christmas Day,*
> *Aw, wouldn't we have a time, baby?*

During the ten years after Johnson's death, a group of younger bluesmen from Mississippi migrated to Chicago, where they developed the bar blues style of rhythm and blues. Many black people had moved to northern cities to take advantage of the good-paying factory work that became available at the outbreak of World War II. But Chicago was the city where the Mississippi blues would flourish most.

Singers like Muddy Waters, Elmore James, and Howlin' Wolf began using electric guitars and adding other instruments, usually piano, bass, and drums. This new, fuller and louder version of the blues was more suitable for dancing than the acoustic guitar accompaniment of the rural blues singers. These noisier, more raucous sounds also seemed to better reflect the pace of life in the big city.

In 1947, Muddy Waters became the first of this new group of Mississippi-Chicago blues singers to record commercially. Several years earlier, the folklorist Alan Lomax had gone down to Mississippi looking for Robert Johnson, who had been dead for a number of years. Lomax did find Muddy Waters, however, and cut several sides for the Library of Congress. These cuts were a far cry from the Muddy Waters who became the king of the Chicago blues, the man Eric Clapton considers his spiritual father, the musician whose sound Keith Richards called "The thing I was looking for, the thing that pulled it all together for me."

During the late forties, Muddy and his band became legendary on the Chicago blues scene. But it wasn't until the early fifties that they started having rhythm and blues hits like "Rollin' Stone," "Hoochie Coochie Man," and "Just Make Love to Me." Here's how author Charlie Gillett described Muddy's uniquely powerful music in *The Sound Of The City:*

Waters rarely "sang" but contented himself with a rough shout, spitting and muttering with a harshness which had no parallels in recorded music. In part, the rawness reflected the spirit of the bars where Waters formed his style. [These places] were rowdy with the laughter, shouts and loud conversation of the drinkers, with whose noise the band had to compete. Melody and harmony as conventionally understood were irrelevant; [Muddy Waters's music] shot emotion at its audience in heavy loads.

In spite of Muddy's tremendous musicianship and his reputation among blues audiences, few of his records made the R&B top ten after the mid-fifties. Black audiences wanted a lighter, less gruff sound than what Muddy and his band were offering. It took a concert tour of England in 1958 to reignite Muddy's career. "I had to go to England to get here," Muddy once said, and it was true. Mick Jagger recalled the effect the great bluesman had on British musicians. As he told an interviewer on Chicago radio station WXRT-FM:

When Muddy Waters came to England in 1958, he shocked the English public by coming out and playing electric guitars and electric basses and electric harmonicas. Instead of a sultry Negro man playing the blues—which is what those English people paid for—he came out with the band and made a deafening noise. . . . This was a great moment because it showed that Muddy Waters was an *electric* blues band. . . .

When Muddy and his band played the Newport Folk Festival in 1960, he captured a whole new American audience with his rendition of "Got My

Mojo Working." From that point on, Muddy lived a relatively secure life for a blues musician. Still, he never made big money or received the notoriety of an Eric Clapton or a Mick Jagger. By the time Muddy was able to attract audiences at some of the larger rock concert halls, he was in his mid-fifties and past his prime.

In 1969, I played in a blues band that opened for Muddy at Philadelphia's Electric Factory. Muddy seemed pleased that younger white musicians idolized him and felt honored just to be in his company. Still, he let his band carry most of the set, coming out to sing on only three or four numbers.

In later years, Muddy proved that he could still turn it on when he wanted to. He gave a particularly rousing performance of "I'm a Man" in the Band's *The Last Waltz* in 1978. But on other nights, he just didn't seem to have the strength or the motivation to really work. Perhaps the years had taken their toll, not to speak of the racism and shady business dealings that had held him down for so long.

Singer Peter Wolf was one of many young white musicians who hung out with Muddy and his band. He remembers how sad it made him to see the hotel his idol had to stay in when he performed in Boston. As Wolf told *Rolling Stone* (a magazine which took its name from a Muddy Waters song):

> [When] I took [Muddy and his band] to their hotel . . . it was a sad, sad story. It was far on the other end of town in the red light district, just one step up from being a flophouse. And here were these men I worshiped checking in. I'll never forget that. That's when I started to get a sense of the great injustice that was going on in

Muddy Waters, king of the Chicago blues singers.

music. . . . To see it so vividly . . . the plaster falling off the walls and the creaky old beds in this fleabitten hotel, and here were these heroic men, these great, great artists.

It's difficult to know just who to blame for this sad state of affairs. We can only imagine how much worse the situation might have been if rock musicians like Eric Clapton and Johnny Winter hadn't spoken of their debt to Muddy and taken a direct interest in his career.

Shortly before Muddy passed away in 1983, he told writer Robert Palmer that this was the best time of his life. When Palmer asked if he harbored any bitterness about the good times taking so long to arrive, Muddy shook his head and said, "Are you kiddin'? I'm glad it came before I died." For many of Muddy's less fortunate contemporaries, it never came. The great Robert Johnson died at age twenty-one, without ever collecting a penny in songwriting royalties. Others, like Son House, migrated to the North but never could make a living in music.

An early idol of both Robert Johnson and Muddy Waters, Son House quit playing music shortly after he moved from the Mississippi Delta to Rochester, New York, at the start of World War II. Like many black people from the South, this seminal bluesman wanted to take advantage of the good wages Northern factories were paying. Son House stayed in the Northeast working, among other things, as a railroad porter. By 1962, he hadn't picked up his guitar in almost fifteen years.

Around this time, there was a growing interest in the blues, and folklorist Alan Lomax asked this Delta blues pioneer to record a few sides for the Library of Congress. There was no pay for the sessions outside of a bottle of cola. But as House jokingly told writer Arnold Shaw, "[at least the cola] was good and cold."

One blues story without a happy ending or humorous punch line is that of Arthur "Big Boy" Cruddup. Though he wrote Elvis Presley's first single, "That's Alright Mamma," he died broke and generally unacknowledged for his contributions. This would seem rather strange, on the surface, because Elvis often spoke of his debt to Big Boy. Furthermore, nobody ever disputed the fact that Cruddup actually wrote the song.

Bobby Robinson, who managed Arthur Cruddup during his last years, remembers his unsuccessful attempts to collect some of the royalties due this deserving songwriter:

> Although Cruddup's name appears on all recordings of "That's Alright Mamma," he never got paid. There was a guy named Lester Melrose who traveled the South and recorded any bluesman he came across on an old wire recorder. He also published the songs these men recorded.
>
> Arthur Cruddup was a migrant farmer—a troubadour who understood nothing about copyrights and royalties. . . . He played and sang here and there, but he had no knowledge of the music business.
>
> At some point, Lester Melrose sold all his publishing rights to a large New York publishing firm, Hill and Range Music. . . . I decided to try and sue Hill and Range because they had never given Cruddup a dime. Songwriting royalties on a Presley record amounted to thousands of dollars a year. Hill and Range finally agreed to make a settlement of about $13,000. Cruddup flew to New York with his sons. This was going to be more money than they had ever seen in their lives.
>
> At the last minute, Hill and Range backed out. They decided that a court settlement probably would cost them less than the $13,000. In the end, Cruddup received something like $1,600. A few years later, he died penniless.

This is a sad but rather typical story of a bluesman getting beat out of his money. It always seems odd that even when someone's contributions are public knowledge, no adjustments can be made. But this is just another legal aspect of the music business that most blues musicians simply were not equipped to handle.

It sometimes seems as if the label *blues singer* was read by some as an advertisement that said: Here is an ignorant person from some rural back country just waiting to be exploited. Give him a bottle, a woman, and a couple of dollars and he'll be content.

Even B.B. King—the most commercially successful blues performer of our time—sometimes feels defensive about this label. As he told Arnold Shaw in *The World of Soul:*

> If Frank Sinatra can be top in his field . . . why can't I be great in blues? Blues isn't dirty. It's American. . . . I would like to be called a singer and be given the same kind of respect for my style that Sinatra gets for his. . . . I don't mind being called a blues singer just so long as the tone of voice is right. . . . [When] a lot of people say "blues singer," you know they're thinking of some ignorant lush moaning in a gutter. . . . There's no reason why a man can't sing the blues as a profession and be a gentleman.

Perhaps B.B. owes part of his great success to the fact that his blues was of a smoother, more sophisticated style than that of Muddy Waters and other bluesmen with rural roots. Though he was born in the Mississippi Delta, B.B. didn't start playing the blues until he entered the army. B.B. talks about how he became a blues musician in the book *Honkers and Shouters:*

> . . . [Before I went into the army] I played mostly spirituals and sang songs I heard in church. I was not trying

to make a living with the guitar, and I was performing things that my family . . . and their friends were familiar with. People of the Sanctified Church thought of the blues as devil songs. But I was listening to the blues from the time . . . I was seven or eight years old. But I didn't start trying to play the blues until I was old enough to go into the service. My buddies were not interested in spirituals. When I came back home, I still would not play the blues around the house. I used to go off on weekends to neighboring towns and play the blues on street corners. Made more money that way than I could collect in a week of picking cotton.

Though B.B. was unusually skilled at farm work—he remembers being one of the top ten tractor drivers in Mississippi—he was determined to make a living in the music business. He started out as a disc jockey, and a few years later was fronting the top band in Memphis. Part of B.B.'s popularity and influence was his single-string guitar style, which evolved out of his own technical limitations. "My coordination wasn't very good," he told Arnold Shaw, "so trying to sing and play at the same time didn't get to me."

While most blues guitarists of that era played a full accompaniment, B.B. only used his guitar to respond or fill in between vocal lines. Singing mostly about troubles with women, B.B. plays his guitar— which he calls "Lucille"—with a delicacy that reflects the influences of jazz musicians like the French guitarist D'Jango Reinhard and the saxophonist Lester Young more than those of rural bluesmen like Robert Johnson and Son House.

B.B.'s vibrant voice, accessible guitar style, and strong commercial sense have helped him forge a popularity that is unique among blues artists. Only B.B. King knows how to maintain the kind of middle ground that makes him pleasing to authentic blues buffs, rock guitarists, middle-American viewers of Johnny Carson's "Tonight" show, and even country music fans. In spite of his broad appeal, however, B.B. classifies himself as a blues or rhythm and blues musician. As he told Arnold Shaw in *Honkers and Shouters:*

> The distinctions that I hear writers make between blues and rhythm and blues I regard as artificial. . . . For instance, James Brown is considered rhythm and blues. Aretha Franklin is considered soul or rhythm and blues—and I am considered blues. . . . I personally think it's all rhythm and blues because it's blues and it has rhythm.

These days, you can sometimes catch B.B. working concerts along with fellow bluesmen Albert King and Bobby "Blue" Bland. Though B.B. receives top billing whenever the three work together, I find Albert King a more accomplished blues guitarist and Bobby Bland a far more gifted and versatile singer. In all fairness, though, it is doubtful that on their own these bluesmen could draw the kind of audiences that fill major concert halls. B.B., on the other hand, has proven that he can bring the people in no matter who the opening acts are. That's why he's always the headliner.

Just as B.B. King used a combination of rural blues, church music, and jazz to forge his unique sound, other musicians were using the same elements and coming up with styles of their own. One style that became popular after World War II was big-band ur-

Bobby "Blue" Bland—perhaps the most
versatile rhythm and blues singer of his generation.

ban blues. During the thirties and forties, famous
black band leaders like Duke Ellington, Count Basie,
and Lionel Hampton established their bands in the
big cities of the North.

This sound was picked up by Glen Miller, the
Dorsey Brothers, and other white bands. By the end
of the war, there were two distinct audiences for big-
band music—listeners (jazz) and dance (rhythm and
blues). Many of the better black bands (including
those mentioned) could play both types of music. But
most of them found it necessary to choose one and
disregard the other.

Ellington, Basie, and Hampton decided to con-
centrate on jazz. But bandleaders like Lucky Millender and Tiny Bradshaw focused on rhythm and

blues. These bands were able to generate tremendous excitement at dances by featuring dynamic singers and strong, screaming tenor sax players who would get down on their knees during solos. In order to survive economically, many of the early rhythm and blues band leaders eventually had to cut down on their personnel. This led to the popularity of the smaller jump combos.

The most important jump combo in terms of both commercial success and influence was Louis Jordan's Tympany Five. Like most of these bands, Jordan's group contained a rhythm section and featured a shouting lead vocalist and a honking saxophone player. Jordan, who sang and played alto saxophone, recorded two big hits in 1945: "Choo Choo Ch' Boogie," and "Caldonia (What Makes Your Big Head So Hard)." Both of these records sold a million copies—appealing to white and black audiences alike.

Jordan sang in a clear and unslurred manner for a blues singer, and used a comic style that was equally entertaining to black and white listeners. His clever, topical approach to songwriting influenced Chuck Berry, while the music and entertaining antics of his combo were models for the first successful rock 'n' roll band—Bill Haley and the Comets. More than any other musician of the late forties and early fifties, Jordan demonstrated the potential of rhythm and blues as a music that would sell to both black and white audiences.

Although space considerations do not permit a discussion of every important blues style and musician, our story would be incomplete without a look at two female blues singers who come out of the so-called *classic blues* tradition.

Though the first professional blues singers were men, the first to get commercially recorded were women. Because of the toughness and danger of the life-style, it was harder for a woman singer than a man to wander from town to southern town trying to eke out a living. Instead, many talented female singers headed for cities where blues were in demand as a form of entertainment. The style that became known as the classic blues was marked by piano rather than guitar accompaniment and an overriding concern with man-woman relationships.

Bessie Smith was the best and most well known of the early classic blues singers. So great was her success that, at the height of her career, she was earning close to two thousand dollars for a personal appearance—a phenomenal sum in the 1920s.

Bessie was a tall, heavyset woman, who turned professional in her teens. She was discovered by an older blues singer named Gertrude (Ma) Rainey. As legend has it, Ma was so impressed with Bessie's singing that she hired her as part of her minstrel troupe. Some say it was to teach her, others claim it was to prevent Bessie from taking over Ma's reign. But it didn't take long for others to discover Bessie. A record company scout spotted her during a minstrel performance in Philadelphia and signed her to a contract.

Bessie cut over a hundred sides in the twenties. Her best-known record is "Downhearted Blues," which sold over a million copies. So terrific was her talent that people ran out of adjectives trying to describe it. Here is how one musician who played with Bessie described her in Nat Hentoff's *Hear Me Talkin' to Ya:*

> Bessie was a fabulous deal to watch. . . . She was a pretty
> large woman and she could sing the blues. . . . You didn't
> turn your head when she went on. You just watched. . . .
> If you had any church background . . . you would recog-
> nize a similarity between what she was doing and what
> those [Southern] . . . preachers did. . . . She could bring
> about a mass hypnotism. When she was performing, you
> could hear a pin drop.

Bessie had a reputation among whites as well as
blacks. But unlike many performers of her era, she
seemed unable or unwilling to cater to the tastes of
white audiences in those days. Such audiences often
looked to black performers for fun and entertainment. But Bessie was something much more: She was
an artist. Writer Tony Palmer describes her power in
his book *All You Need Is Love:*

> [Bessie's] material ranged from intensely poetic blues to
> mediocre pop songs. . . . But . . . she infused everything
> with an unparalleled grandeur and humanity. She
> seemed able to impart the sadness of mortality, the insta-
> bility of happiness, the craving for certainty, [and] the
> self-destructive pursuit of temporary oblivion. . . .

When she wasn't performing, Bessie tried to remain a rather humble and simple person. She had
some well-publicized problems, both with men and
the bottle. By the mid-thirties, her star had fallen. At
her last appearance at Harlem's Apollo Theater, her
fee had dropped to $250. In the end, though, it may
have been racism that killed Bessie Smith.

One night in September 1937, Bessie and her
current lover were driving from Memphis to join a
show in Huntsville, Alabama. Suddenly, a huge truck
approached head-on, and Bessie's car was forced off

Janis Joplin—
Bessie Smith
was her idol.

the narrow road. The facts about what happened
after that are rather confused. But some people close
to the situation claim that Bessie died because she was
refused admittance to an all-white hospital. By the
time she found a doctor who would treat her, she had
lost too much blood to be saved.

In 1970, shortly before her own tragic death,
rock singer Janis Joplin paid tribute to her idol by
contributing money for a new headstone for Bessie's
grave. It read:

THE GREATEST BLUES SINGER IN THE WORLD
WILL NEVER STOP SINGING
BESSIE SMITH
1895–1937

Though Bessie Smith had died, the classic blues tradition still lived through a tortured, phenomenally talented singer named Billie Holiday. Billie was discovered by John Hammond—the same producer who worked with Bessie Smith, and whose amazing list of discoveries includes Aretha Franklin, Bob Dylan, and Bruce Springsteen.

Billie Holiday's career was to span two decades. Her material included blues, pop standards, and songs of social protest. But no matter what the song or musical arrangement, Billie brought a depth of feeling and despair that was shattering in its intensity.

There have been many attempts to explain and interpret Billie's life and music. Though many of the actual facts were glossed over, the 1973 film *Lady Sings the Blues,* with Diana Ross as Billie, captures the essence of her story.

Born into a broken home and brought up in brothels, Billie was jailed for prostitution by the time she was fourteen. Soon she discovered heroin—the substance that both helped her tolerate a painful life and ultimately led her to an early grave.

Billie's music is as painful and haunted as the blues can get, but her sheer musical genius makes it a joy to listen to. She once described her approach to singing this way:

> I don't think I'm singing. I feel like I'm playing a horn. I try to improvise like Lester Young and Louis Armstrong. What comes out is what I feel. I hate straight singing. I have to change a tune to my own way of doing it. That's all I know.

Billie's way of doing a tune has put her high up on the list of all-time great blues singers. This in spite

Billie Holliday. She brought a depth of feeling and despair to her singing that was shattering in its intensity.

of the fact that she did not have a particularly strong voice, nor did she perform many songs that were twelve-bar blues. Yet the feeling in her voice when she sang "My Man" or "God Bless the Child" was the very essence of the blues.

Billie sang only one protest song—"Strange Fruit." One night a schoolteacher named Lewis Allen gave her a poem he had written. The words were about the lynching of blacks in the South. When Billie realized what the words "strange fruit hanging from the poplar trees" meant, she wasn't sure whether she should include it in her act. "I was scared that people would hate it," she said at the time:

53

> The first time I sang ["Strange Fruit"] I thought it was a mistake and I had been right being scared. There wasn't even a patter of applause when I finished. Then a lone person began to clap nervously. Then suddenly everyone was clapping.

In essence, Billie Holiday was the last of the great classic blues singers. Her whole life—and her music—seemed to be based on feelings of infinite sadness and a sense of irretrievable loss. Her producer, John Hammond, remembers that Billie took the death of her mother particularly hard. As he told writer Tony Palmer:

> [After her mother died, Billie] went from one terrible guy to another. . . . She never had any luck with men, although she had some extraordinary men working flat out to help her. . . . Billie abused her voice—and herself. There was only a shred of her voice left before she died.

When Billie Holiday passed away in 1959, her friends and associates were saddened, but few were surprised. Tony Palmer characterizes Billie's place in blues history this way:

> Billie Holiday was the singer whose life . . . [was] a constant reminder of what the blues was and had been. Her art was exquisite and unique, her voice spilling over with rough melancholy, expressing a sorrow too deep for words. She spoke for countless generations who had suffered; but equally she spoke for others, with heroic pessimism, about love abandoned, love forgotten, love denied and love rejected. She touched a chord beyond race or creed or time. And yet, she was utterly of her race and her creed and her time. . . .

Two years before her death, Billie Holiday told an interviewer from *Time* magazine how she felt about the blues: "To me, the blues are like being very sad, very sick—and again like going to church and being very happy." Perhaps this dual nature of blues and blues-based music lends a clue to its lasting appeal and popularity.

What other music is versatile enough to express both heartbreak and laughter, suitable for both serious listening and carefree dancing, adaptable to both searing electric guitars and smoldering female vocalists? Writer Langston Hughes summarized the complex emotional nature of the blues in his book *Famous Negro Music Makers:*

> The blues are mostly very sad songs about being without love, without money or without a home. And yet almost always in the blues, there is some humorous twist of thought, in words that make people laugh. . . . The music is slow, often mournful, yet syncopated, with the kind of marching bass behind it that seems to say, "In spite of fate, bad luck, these blues themselves, I'm going on! I'm going to get there."

## SELECTED DISCOGRAPHY

### BOBBY "BLUE" BLAND
*Best of Bobby "Blue" Bland* . . . . . . . . . . . . . . . . . . . . . . . . Duke
*Best of Bobby "Blue" Bland—Volume 2* . . . . . . . . . . . . . . . . Duke
*Introspective of the Early Years* . . . . . . . . . . . . . . . . . . . . . Duke

### BIG BILL BROONZY
*Big Bill Broonzy Memorial* . . . . . . . . . . . . . . . . . . . . . . . . Mercury
*Big Bill Broonzy Story* . . . . . . . . . . . . . . . . . . . . . . . . . . . Verve MG
*Blues with Big Bill Broonzy, Sonny Terry and Brownie McGhee*
Folkways
*Remembering Big Bill* . . . . . . . . . . . . . . . . . . . . . . . . . . . Mercury
*The Young Bill Broonzy* . . . . . . . . . . . . . . . . . . . . . . . . . . Yazoo

## ERIC CLAPTON

Blues Breakers with John Mayall. . . . . . . . . . . . . . . . . . London
Wheels of Fire. . . . . . . . . . . . . . . . . . . . . . . . . . . . . . . . . . . Atco

## ARTHUR BIG BOY CRUDDUP

Mean Ol' Frisco-Fire . . . . . . . . . . . . . . . . . . . . . . . . . . . . Trip
The Father of Rock and Roll . . . . . . . . . . . . . . . . . . . . . . . RCA

## BILLIE HOLIDAY

Billie Holiday Sings. . . . . . . . . . . . . . . . . . . . . . . . . . . . . . Kent
Billie Holiday Story. . . . . . . . . . . . . . . . . . . . . . . . . . . . . . Decca
The Golden Years, Volumes I, II, and III . . . . . . . . . . . . Columbia
The History of the Real Billie Holiday. . . . . . . . . . . . . . . . Verve

## JOHN LEE HOOKER

The Best of John Lee Hooker . . . . . . . . . . . . . . . . . . . . . . Vee Jay
Boogie Chillun. . . . . . . . . . . . . . . . . . . . . . . . . . . . . . . . . . Fantasy
The Greatest Hits . . . . . . . . . . . . . . . . . . . . . . . . . . . . . . . Kent
John Lee Hooker Gold . . . . . . . . . . . . . . . . . . . . . . . . . . . Vee Jay

## SON HOUSE

Delta Blues with J. D. Short . . . . . . . . . . . . . . . . . . . . . . Folkways
The Legendary—1941–42 . . . . . . . . . . . . . . . . . Arhoolie/Folklyric
The Real Delta Blues. . . . . . . . . . . . . . . . . . . . . . . . . . . . Blue Goose
Walking Blues with Willie Brown and Others . . . . . . . . Folk Blues

## HOWLIN' WOLF

Chester Burnett AKA Howlin' Wolf . . . . . . . . . . . . . . . . . . Chess
Howlin' Wolf—Original Folk Blues. . . . . . . . . . . . . . . . . . United
The Legendary Sun Performers . . . . . . . . . . . . . . . . . . . . . Charly
Moaning in the Moonlight (reissued as Evil) . . . . . . . . . . . Chess

## ELMORE JAMES

The Best of Elmore James . . . . . . . . . . . . . . . . . . . . . . . . . . Sue
The History of Elmore James . . . . . . . . . . . . . . . . . . . . . . . . Trip
The History of Elmore James Volume II. . . . . . . . . . . . . . . . Trip
The Legend of Elmore James . . . . . . . . . . . . . . . . Kent and United
Original Folk Blues . . . . . . . . . . . . . . . . . . . . . . . . . . . . . . United

## BLIND LEMON JEFFERSON
*Blind Lemon Jefferson 1926–29* . . . . . . . . . . . . . . . . . . Biograph
*The Classic Folk Blues of Blind Lemon Jefferson and Son House*
Biograph

## ROBERT JOHNSON
*The Complete Robert Johnson* . . . . . . . . . . . . . . . . . . . . Columbia
*King of the Delta Blues Singers—Volumes I and II* . . . . Columbia

## LOUIS JORDAN
*Blues Spectrum* . . . . . . . . . . . . . . . . . . . . . . . . . . . . . . . . . Decca
*Let the Good Times Roll* . . . . . . . . . . . . . . . . . . . . . . . . . Decca

## ALBERT KING
*King of the Blues Guitar* . . . . . . . . . . . . . . . . . . . . French Atlantic
*Live Wire-Blues Power* . . . . . . . . . . . . . . . . . . . . . . . . . . . . . Stax
*Travelin' to California* . . . . . . . . . . . . . . . . . . . . . . . . . . . . . King

## B.B. KING
*B.B. King—1949–50* . . . . . . . . . . . . . . . . . . . . . . . . . . . . . . Kent
*The Best of B.B. King* . . . . . . . . . . . . . . . . . . . . . . . . . . . . . ABC
*Live at the Royal* . . . . . . . . . . . . . . . . . . . . . . . . . . . . . . . . ABC

## LUCKY MILLENDER
*Lucky Millender* . . . . . . . . . . . . . . . . . . . . . . . . . . . . . . . . . Todd

## GERTRUDE "MA" RAINEY
*Immortal Ma Rainey* . . . . . . . . . . . . . . . . . . . . . . . . . . . Milestone

## BESSIE SMITH
*The Bessie Smith Story* . . . . . . . . . . . . . . . . . . . . . . . . . Columbia
*The World's Greatest Blues Singer* . . . . . . . . . . . . . . . . Columbia

## MUDDY WATERS
*The Best of Muddy Waters* . . . . . . . . . . . . . . . . . . . . . . . . Chess
*Down on Stovall's Plantation* . . . . . . . . . . . . . . . . . . . Testament
*McKinley Morganfield AKA Muddy Waters* . . . . . . . . . . . . . Chess
*Muddy "Mississippi" Waters Live* . . . . . . . . . . . . . . . . . Blue Sky
*Sail On* (also issued as *Best of Muddy Waters Down Home*)
Chess
*Super Blues with Bo Diddley and Little Walter* . . . . . . . . . . Chess

# CHAPTER 4

# GOSPEL MUSIC IN AND OUT OF CHURCH

*Gospel music is exactly the same as blues and rhythm and blues, no different. It is the authentic, black expression. You could take the same music and the same beat and say—"oh Lord"—or you can say "oh baby." One is praising God and one is sinful. Where I grew up in the South, that's how old people explained it to the kids—the devil's music and the Lord's music. But it's really all the same thing—authentic black music."*

—Bobby Robinson, rhythm and blues/gospel record producer and songwriter

The blues was traditionally considered to be a somewhat vulgar and disrespectful music by many God-fearing black folks. Although the musical roots of both blues and gospel singing were similar, the social attitudes they represented were thought to be as different as God and the devil. If you wanted to live a life that was good and righteous, you did your singing in church.

The black church, particularly in the South, was the center of most political, economic, and cultural activities. Southern churches were segregated, and

The Staples Singers—extending the audience for music rooted in the black church.

this gave black people the opportunity to discuss their problems and express their feelings openly, without interference from whites. As Charlie Gillett put it in *The Sound of the City:*

> . . . People who valued their place in the Negro—and American—society wisely chose to sing in church. To the outside world, this seemed to be an admirably conventional thing to do—accepting one of the society's most sturdy institutions, the church of God. And perhaps it seemed too that if everybody believed in God, they would accept the way He had planned the world, which included some unequal distributions of wealth, happiness and opportunity.

Many astute blacks recognized that the church offered a meeting ground—a center for change and action. It is no coincidence, then, that some of our most important black political leaders began their careers in the church. One only has to listen to the oratory style of the Reverend Jesse Jackson to see how magnificently preaching ability and political astuteness can mix.

A great number of our finest black singers began their careers in church. Some, like Mahalia Jackson and James Cleveland, never ventured into the world of popular music. But others, like Sam Cooke and Aretha Franklin, had successful commercial careers after building reputations in the religious community.

For the average black in the South, though, the church was not a means to a career in either politics or music. People sometimes lived miles from their closest neighbor, and the church provided a social center. Church singing was a good way to get together with friends and let out your feelings—maybe have a little fun. Since there was no television, very few radios, and little money for other forms of amusement, people sang to entertain themselves. Bobby Robinson remembers how it was in those days. In fact, his early experiences in the Southern church community inspired him to go on to become one of our most important rhythm and blues record producers. Robinson's long list of hits includes Gladys Knight and the Pips' "Every Beat Of My Heart," Wilbert Harrison's "Kansas City," Lee Dorsey's "Ya Ya," and the Channels' "The Closer You Are." His work stretches from seminal bluesmen like Arthur Cruddup and Elmore James to contemporary rap artists like Grand Master Flash. Still, with all the music he's been involved with over the years, Bobby Robinson lights up when he recalls his musical beginnings:

> When I was a kid in the South, every church community had a half dozen singing groups. In fact, my cousins and I had one of these groups. Since there was no instrumental backing, the groups had to compensate with a strong vocal sound. These gospel-based groups were the forerunners of the street-corner vocal groups that became popular in the fifties.

The music that came out of these Southern churches was at least as important as the blues in shaping contemporary rhythm and blues, jazz, and much of the better rock music. Many accomplished black singers were capable of singing blues as well as gospel, but the church frowned upon blues singing. To many blacks, the blues meant resigning yourself to the conditions of slavery and social oppression. The music of the church, on the other hand, offered hope

for something better—if not in this life, then in the
hereafter.

"Blues are the songs of despair," Mahalia Jackson
once said. "Gospel songs are the songs of hope. When
you sing gospel, you have the feeling that there is a
cure for what's wrong. . . ."

Many churchgoing blacks had an even more important objection to blues singing. They saw it as the
devil's music, a bottomless pit that could only lead to a
shiftless, immoral life of drinking and promiscuous
sex. Gospel, on the other hand, was the music of eternal goodness and salvation.

Bobby Robinson recalls that, as a teenager growing up in South Carolina, he was warned by his parents that the blues was an evil music. Still, there was
something about this forbidden fruit that he just had
to taste.

Mahalia Jackson—never
strayed from her gospel roots.

As a kid, I used to slip off and go to what they call country frolics. These older guys would pick me up and we'd drive into the hills. There were bootleggers and whisky drinkers. Some guy would go in the backyard and pull a bottle of white lightning out. It was ten cents a glass. When you gobbled it down, your hat would almost come off your head. My mother didn't allow me to go around those kind of people and I'd always get a whipping when I came home. But I heard something. I didn't know what it was, but something inside me was driving me on. I had to know and identify with the source of the blues . . . I had heard it on the street corners from vendors hawking wares, and I heard the guys in the field sing. But going to these forbidden places and hearing the real blues was something that everyone there related to because they knew it was music of a common experience.

On Saturday nights, these hardworking country people would dress up in their overalls and shine their shoes. They'd get up on the floor and turn their cap backwards. And they would be "partying hard"—as the people say—to this music. I was fascinated watching these guys sing, dance and make love to their women. That's what the real country blues was like in its early days.

Even today, the blues are still frowned upon in certain corners of the black community. In the Mississippi Delta and other areas of the rural South, musicians who are skilled in both styles still harbor their own deep-rooted fears of mixing blues with gospel. As blues performer James "Son" Thomas told writer William Ferris in *The Delta Blues:*

If I go to church and pray and sing church songs, and [then] I leave there and go to a [bar] and play blues, I think that's where the wrongness comes in. You ain't supposed to cross them that way. I'd be afraid to do that 'cause something bad can happen to you. That's what you call going too far wrong. You can't serve the Lord and the Devil too.

Not all blues singers believe their music is sinful. They particularly resent being called evil by preachers who drink and otherwise lead lives that go against religious teachings. One Delta bluesman told William Ferris that "a blues performer is more honorable than . . . [such] hypocritical preachers . . . because the bluesman's music openly states the teachings by which he lives." Bluesman Son House once wrote a song that expressed these sentiments:

> *Oh, I'm gonna get me religion,*
> *I'm gonna join the Baptist Church.*
> *Oh, I'm gonna get me religion,*
> *I'm gonna join the Baptist Church.*
> *I'm gonna be a Baptist preacher,*
> *And I sure won't have to work.*

Preachers and devoted churchgoers are no less skeptical and resentful of blues musicians. They are especially upset by those who use elements of gospel music or use the Lord's name in their music. "Many are taught from childhood that the bluesman is the 'devil's preacher,'" notes William Ferris. "When the blues strike a religious person, he should go off, sing the blues and then ask forgiveness. But under no circumstances should the two musics be mixed."

If, for financial reasons, a gospel singer wants to perform at a blues club, he or she sometimes has to do so on the sneak. In the fifties, Gladys Knight and the Pips were one of many groups to lead this kind of double musical life. Before they started making hit records, they worked clubs in Atlanta, Georgia, as the Pips, but used a different name for their gospel work. Once their records made the charts, though, they were through as gospel performers.

To assume a dual musical identity was virtually impossible for singers who were already nationally recognized gospel stars. If an established religious performer dared to make a popular record, he risked losing his audience. Bobby Robinson remembers how hesitant the great Sam Cooke was about making popular recordings:

> Before he became a famous pop singer, Sam Cooke was a member of the Soul Stirrers. That group was extremely popular even before Sam joined them. Sam's father was a storefront preacher in Chicago who used to have his family back him up. Sam was just a teenager, but when the members of the Soul Stirrers heard him sing, they convinced his old man to let him join the group. Sam was so young and such a natural talent, that the Soul Stirrers soon became one of the most popular gospel groups in the country.
>
> I knew Sam and the rest of the Soul Stirrers pretty well. I knew he had the makings of a tremendous popular star and I was trying to convince him to make the move. One night, I went back to his room at the Cecil Hotel in Harlem. He said he had this original song that he wanted to play for me. The room was crowded with girls and fellas, so me and Sam went into the men's room. We locked the door and Sam played "You Send Me" while he accompanied himself on acoustic guitar.
>
> After I heard him sing "You Send Me," I said, "Make the move right now. You've got an original sound that hasn't been heard yet in popular music. There are guys copying your sound. They're sitting in their rooms night and day and trying to imitate what you do. The first one

The Soul-Stirrers (Sam Cooke, front). They created some of
the greatest vocal music ever heard in or out of church.

to hit the street is going to make it big, and it will be too
late for you." He said, "Bobby, I'm making two hundred
dollars a week, which supports my family. The gospel
audience is funny. They consider me a religious person.
If I become a pop singer and fail, they might not take
me back. What will I do then, take a broom and sweep
the streets?"

A few weeks later Sam Cooke recorded "You
Send Me"—the first of a long series of popular hits.
Other gospel stars who had opportunities to make
popular records chose to stick with church music.

Mahalia Jackson refused many lucrative offers to sing in nightclubs. "The church will be here when the nightclubs are gone," she once remarked.

When Mahalia Jackson—hailed as the greatest gospel singer of her generation—began recording gospel hits in 1945, she established the previously untapped commercial potential for this kind of black religious singing. By the end of World War II, millions of blacks had moved from the rural South to ghetto communities in the North and Midwest. This migration corresponded with the rise of hundreds of black storefront churches, and with the growing popularity of professional gospel singers.

Between 1945 and 1950, many companies that had recorded rhythm and blues also began releasing a considerable number of gospel records—often on a label with a different name. Some of the important performers to be recorded during this period were Marie Knight, Rosetta Tharpe, the Dixie Hummingbirds, the Silvertone Singers, the Pilgrim Travelers, and the Five Blind Boys of Mississippi.

These gospel singers handled emotion in a different manner than most blues singers. The blues is often a more detached, musical form in which the singer/narrator *tells* of his or her troubles. But gospel is a music that requires complete emotional involvement.

Writer James Baldwin, once a preacher in a Harlem storefront church, describes the intensity of gospel in his book *The Fire Next Time:*

> There is no music like that music, no drama like the drama of the saints rejoicing, the sinners moaning, the tambourines racing, and all those voices crying together and crying holy unto the Lord. I have never seen any-

thing to equal the fire and excitement that sometimes, without warning, fill a church, causing a church to . . . "rock." Nothing that has happened to me since equals the power and the glory that I sometimes felt when . . . the church I were one. . . .

There was a zest and a joy and a capacity for facing and surviving disaster that are very moving and very rare. Perhaps we were all of us—pimps, whores, racketeers, church members, and children—bound together by the nature of our oppression. If so, within these limits we sometimes achieved with each other a freedom that was close to love. . . . This is the freedom that one hears in some gospel songs.

This is also the freedom you can feel in Little Richard's music. You can call songs like "Long Tall Sally," "Rip It Up," and "Lucille" rock 'n' roll, blues, or rhythm and blues. But Bobby Robinson calls it "the Baptist beat":

Little Richard made the same kind of music as the Baptist church congregations. In churches throughout the South, we call this "the Baptist beat." Those churches were too poor to even have a piano or organ, but the music was the greatest I ever heard in my whole life.

The Baptist beat was really electric. It would start with a single hand clap and move to a double hand clap. That's the same beat that is used in rock 'n' roll. Little Richard used his band to do the same things the congregation was doing with their hands, feet and voices. Of course, he changed the words to suit the kids. But if you ever go into a Southern Baptist church, you'll hear the same kind of feel.

While Little Richard was instrumental in bringing a gospel fervor to popular music, his bizarre lifestyle has come to symbolize the conflict between the blues and religious outlooks. For over twenty-five years now, he has been alternating between a life of flashy clothes, homosexuality, and drug abuse, and one of preaching. A sermon from one of Richard's more recent transitions to the side of good is quoted in his autobiography, *The Life and Times of Little Richard, the Quasar of Rock:*

> I want to say, "Hello out there. I'm so glad to be with you today. My name is Little Richard. I'm the rock & roll singer that you've heard about through the years. I was making $10,000 for one hour. Just jumping up in the air with all of the makeup and eyelashes on. With all of the mirrored suits and the sequins and the stones going all over the place. I had forgotten all about God. Going from town to town, country to country, not knowing that I was directed and commanded by another power. The power of darkness. The power that you've heard so much about. The power that a lot of people don't believe exists. The power of the Devil.
>
> I gave up rock & roll for the rock of ages. I cut off my crown of hair for a crown of life. . . . God saved Little Richard.

On the whole, rhythm and blues performers who incorporated gospel music into their work weren't experiencing the emotional and moral turmoil of a Little Richard. Some of them weren't even particularly religious. The question for most singers wasn't so much one of right or wrong, but of finding a commercial style that would sell records.

Ray Charles had been searching for a commercially viable style for years before he hit on the idea of combining gospel music with blues lyrics. He once said, "The blues and gospel are pretty much the same. The main difference is that in the blues you're singing 'oh baby' and in gospel you're singing 'oh Lord.' "

With that in mind, he took the gospel classic, "This Little Light of Mine," and changed it to "This Little Girl of Mine." "My Jesus is All the World to Me" became "I Got A Woman." Ray Charles had done something that was considered unthinkable in 1955— he had taken gospel music and turned it into dance music. All the elements of gospel were there, the rhythms, the call-and-response singing, and the emotional fervor. But the object of the singer's joy was not God, but a woman. Ray Charles's records were now attracting a large white audience, but gospel-tinged music was already familiar to black listeners.

In 1950, the Dominoes became the first group of black gospel-trained singers to make a popular record. The group was formed by Billy Ward, a New York–based piano player and singing instructor. The group's lead singer was Clyde McPhatter. The Dominoes' first hit was "Sixty Minute Man," which featured bass singer Bill Brown boasting about his skill as a lover. This record was followed on the R&B charts by two other hits, "Have Mercy Baby," and "The Bells." Both of these songs featured McPhatter's high, smooth gospel voice. When he left the group to form the Drifters in 1953, the Dominoes' lead singing chores were taken over by Jackie Wilson, another strong gospel-type singer.

Because of the Dominoes' popularity, many other groups began to record gospel-influenced material. The Five Royals were one of the better and more successful of these. Originally a straight gospel group that recorded as the Royal Sons Quintet, the Five Royals had several R&B hits on the Apollo label:

"Baby Don't Do It," and "Help Me Somebody." After moving to the King label in the late fifties, the group had two more hits that became well known, "Think," and "Dedicated to the One I Love." Although the Five Royals were not as famous as the Dominoes or the early Drifters, their best records are fine examples of early gospel-influenced R&B.

In 1954, the gospel sound started making its presence felt on the upper reaches of the R&B charts. The most important gospel-style group of that year was Hank Ballard and the Midnighters. The group had three top ten R&B hits that year: "Work With Me

Ray Charles—instead of saying "oh, Lord," he said "oh, baby!"

Annie," "Sexy Ways," and "Annie Had A Baby." All three songs were full of explicit sexual references, and all three were cited as objectionable by civic groups like the Houston Juvenile Delinquency and Crime Commission.

Black audiences found the Midnighters' records both amusing and danceable. While Ballard sang the humorously suggestive lyrics in a plaintive and serious tone, the rest of the group supplied a rich and rhythmic vocal support. Though "Work With Me Annie" was dubbed "the black national anthem of 1954," the record and its follow-ups were banned by white stations.

By the late fifties, many gospel-influenced records had sold well to white and black listeners alike. The commercial potential of gospel music had been explored by James Brown, Ray Charles, Jackie Wilson, Sam Cooke, the Isley Brothers, and others. And this was only the beginning. During the next few years, gospel techniques such as hand clapping, call-and-response singing, and tambourine playing became standard features on all kinds of popular records.

In the mid-sixties, gospel and rhythm and blues was forged into a unique mixture known as *soul*. Although the word *soul* has been employed by music industry trade publications in recent years to mean black popular styles, the term was originally coined to describe those records and performers who used the fervor of gospel to express social protest and other worldly concerns. As Arnold Shaw notes in *The World of Soul*, the widespread use of gospel in soul music came at a time when blacks were experiencing a growing sense of pride in themselves.

. . . Blues was natural in an era when Negroes felt that they *had* to bear whatever burdens were imposed upon them. . . . Soul is a [product] of a time when they are unafraid to shout out their grievances and determined to throw off unjust burdens.

If you listen to the infectious spirit of gospel, it is not hard to understand why this music spread its power and energy beyond strictly religious confines. Gospel had started out as the music of an oppressed people making "a joyful noise unto the heavens." Only a few short decades after its commercial implications had begun to be explored, gospel had evolved into a worldly music that celebrated new possibilities for happiness and freedom—not just in heaven, but also right here on earth.

## GOSPEL SELECTED DISCOGRAPHY

### HANK BALLARD AND THE MIDNIGHTERS
*Hank Ballard and the Midnighters* . . . . . . Starday and Powerpak
*Hank Ballard's Greatest Juke Box Hits* . . . . . . . . . . . . . . . . King
*Spotlight on Hank Ballard* . . . . . . . . . . . . . . . . . . Starday Gusto

### JAMES BROWN
*At the Apollo* . . . . . . . . . . . . . . . . . . . . . . . . . . . . . . . . . . . . . Polydor
*The Best of James Brown* . . . . . . . . . . . . . . . . . . . . . . . . . Polydor
*Say It Loud—I'm Black and I'm Proud* . . . . . . . . . . . . . . . . . King
*Soul Classics—Volumes I, II, and III* . . . . . . . . . . . . . . . . . Polydor
*Twenty-Two Giant Hits* . . . . . . . . . . . . . . . . . . . . . . . . . . . Smash
*Unbeatable Hits* . . . . . . . . . . . . . . . . . . . . . . . . . . . . . . . . . . King

### RAY CHARLES
*Ray Charles's Greatest Hits* . . . . . . . . . . . . . . . . ABC Paramount
*The Ray Charles Story—Volumes I, II, and III* . . . . . . . . . . Atlantic
*The Genuis of Ray Charles* . . . . . . . . . . . . . . . . . . . . . . . . Atlantic
*What'd I Say* . . . . . . . . . . . . . . . . . . . . . . . . . . . . . . . . . . . Atlantic
*25th Anniversary* . . . . . . . . . . . . . . . . . . . . . . . . . . . . . . . . . . ABC

Billy Ward and his
Dominoes, Hank Ballard
and the Midnighters,
the Isley Brothers,
the Five Royales.

## JAMES CLEVELAND

James Cleveland with the Angelic Choir .............. Savoy

He Leadeth Me with the Cleveland Singers ........... Savoy

## SAM COOKE

The Best of Sam Cooke—Volumes I and II ......... RCA Victor

Sam Cooke Sings.................................... Keen

Gospel Soul of Sam Cooke—Volumes I and II ........ Specialty

Man Who Invented Soul............................. RCA

Original with the Soul Stirrers................... Speciality

16 Greatest Hits..................................... Trip

Shake ............................................. RCA

Unforgettable Sam Cooke ...................... RCA Victor

## BILLY WARD AND THE DOMINOES

Yours Forever.................................... Federal

## FIVE BLIND BOYS OF MISSISSIPPI

The Best of the Five Blind Boys of Mississippi ......... Peacock

## ARETHA FRANKLIN

Amazing Grace with James Cleveland ............. Atlantic

Gospel Soul ...................................... Cheder

Songs of Faith ................................. Columbia

## MAHALIA JACKSON

The World's Greatest Gospel Singer ............... Columbia

## LITTLE RICHARD

The Best of Little Richard........................ Scepter

Greatest Hits..................................... United

Greatest Hits Live ................................ Okeh

King of Gospel Songs............................. Mercury

Here's Little Richard ........................... Speciality

Sings Gospel..................................... Stateside

Sings Spirituals .................................. United

Star Collection .................................. Reprise

20 Original Hits ................................ Specialty

The Very Best of Little Richard ................. United Artists

## CLYDE MCPHATTER
The Best of Clyde McPhatter......................Atlantic
Clyde McPhatter and the Drifters...................Atlantic
Clyde McPhatter with Billy Ward and The Dominoes.......King
Golden Blues Hits..............................Mercury
Greatest Hits..................................Mercury
Greatest Hits.......................................MGM

## THE PILGRIM TRAVELERS
Everytime I Feel the Spirit........................Vee Jay

## THE FIVE ROYALS
All the Hits........................................King
Dedicated to You ..................................King
18 King-Size R&B Hits..........................Columbia
Five Royals.........................................King
Rockin' .........................................Apollo

## SISTER ROSETTA THORPE
Gospel Train .....................................Decca
Precious Lord .....................................Savoy

## JACKIE WILSON
Golden Favorites...............................Brunswick
Greatest Hits..................................Brunswick
World's Greatest Melodies ......................Brunswick

# CHAPTER 5

# WHATEVER HAPPENED TO THE FABULOUS FIFTIES?

*The blues had a baby, and they called it rock 'n' roll.*

—Muddy Waters

Rhythm and blues in the fifties had its own character. It was a music of fantasy, and dreams, and good times. There was something so fresh and rhythmic about this music. Somehow, it had more life to it than anything else on the radio. Even in the most segregated areas of the South, white teenagers were buying thousands of "race records," and rich white ladies were sending their black maids into record stores to do the same.

People who grew up with this music can sometimes close their eyes and remember the first time they heard slow, lovesick records like "The Great Pretender" by the Platters, or "In the Still of the Night" by the Five Satins; or fast, rollicking records like "Long Tall Sally" by Little Richard, or "I'm Walkin'" by Fats Domino. They all sounded great back then, and even today, many of those records still sound great. No social relevance, no references to drugs. Just simple, uncluttered, timeless expressions of real emotion.

Back then, people got to see their favorite performers live. On Christmas and Easter vacations, you could line up by the Brooklyn Paramount and see maybe fifteen of the hottest rock 'n' rollers on the same stage: Chuck Berry, Bo Diddley, Screamin' Jay Hawkins, Jerry Lee Lewis, Frankie Lymon and the Teenagers, the Cleftones, the Harptones, the Del Vikings and more. No mail-order tickets in advance, no scalpers asking two hundred dollars a seat. Just get there early and try to sit as close to the stage as possible so you could hear the music above the screaming girls.

Back then, you took it for granted when just about every group sounded as good as their records. Many of them had, after all, formed their sound on street corners and in hallways. Their recordings were low-budget affairs, so what you heard on the records was usually what you got in person.

When you came home after one of these shows, you felt as if you had taken part in some kind of religious ritual. Later on, you'd find out that this music actually did have its roots in church— particularly the group singing. But then, it was a natural form of expression. Whenever a few guys got together, there was likely to be an attempt at singing. The guy with the closest thing to an in-tune voice would sing: "Oh what a ni-i-ight."

"Doo, doo, doo," the guy with the lowest voice would cut in.

"To kiss you dear," the chorus would chime in.

Every now and then, a neighborhood group would discover that they had some talent and wind up making a record. It wasn't the hardest thing in the world in those days. Thirteen- and fourteen-year-old kids were becoming big stars overnight. Frankie Lymon was one of them—definitely the main one in 1957.

Bobby Robinson shakes his head when he thinks about how close he came to signing Frankie and producing his first and biggest hit, "Why Do Fools Fall in Love":

> A friend of mine, Richard Barrett, told me that there was this singing group up at P.S. 165 in Harlem with a dynamite lead singer. "Let me bring them down to your place after school for just five minutes," he said. "They do a number called 'Why Do Fools Fall in Love' that makes the kids go wild."
>
> I told him to bring them down to my place. But unfortunately, I had some business in Jersey and got detained in traffic. I was only about fifteen minutes late, but the kids were getting restless, so Richard took them to see another producer, George Goldner. Within a couple of hours, Goldner hired a few musicians and cut the record. The group sang the song exactly like they did it in the school auditorium and it became a huge hit.

Frankie Lymon's brother Louie was only ten in 1957. But Bobby Robinson wanted to give Louie a shot—mostly because of his physical and vocal resemblance to Frankie. After all, it only cost a few hundred dollars back then to cut a single. A drummer, piano, guitar, Fender bass, and maybe a sax player were all you needed. A producer could hire musicians for fifty

Frankie Lymon (center) and the Teenagers.

or seventy-five dollars and lay the tracks to a half
dozen tunes. If any of them generated even a little
airplay, you were way ahead of the game.

Louie Lymon's first record for Bobby Robinson
—"I'm So Happy"—was a minor hit in 1957. Unfortunately, Louie didn't have much of a music career
after that. He was just another one-shot recording
act, one of hundreds who made a couple of records,
then disappeared into oblivion.

Frankie was a different story, of course. He was
big for a whole year—the hottest young male soprano
around. His sound was special and so were his records—up-tempo with ballad soul. But Frankie's
career was mishandled. He was ripped off and then
discarded by the entire record industry.

Frankie Lymon was only in his early twenties in the mid-sixties, but he was a has-been. There he was, working some dive in Brooklyn—strung out on drugs, and reminding the musicians of how lucky they were to be backing up the great Frankie Lymon. A few months later, Frankie died of a drug overdose.

Fifteen years had passed since Frankie's death, but he had been so big at one time that they still used his name to sell tickets in 1982.

Twenty-five years is a long time—an eternity in the record business. Ten-year-old Louie Lymon was thirty-five in 1982. His soprano voice and music career were well behind him. Still, they were calling him to work a big oldies show. Could you really blame Louie for wanting one more try at the brass ring?

"No sweat," the promoter tells him. "All you'll need is a quick run-through with the band. Hey, you'll sing Frankie's hits, 'Why Do Fools,' 'The ABC's of Love,' 'I Promise to Remember.' Give the people what they want. The other guys in the group can each take a number. The crowd will love it. Guaranteed! How many of the groups have their original lead singers anyway?"

Nobody knows what Louie was on that night. But he was so smashed that yet another Lymon brother had to take over the lead singing after the third song. And this guy had never even been a one-shot wonder in the fifties. How, I wondered, could they destroy such wonderful music? Why couldn't they just let Frankie Lymon rest in peace and Louie Lymon live with his memories? Even before I asked, I knew that there was a single answer to my questions: *dollars!*

Money has always been a tremendous force in determining the course of popular music. Even back in the early fifties, business people who actually appreciated rhythm and blues understood that if this music was going to sell to white audiences, it needed a new name. That's where rock 'n' roll came in.

Before 1954, the popular music field was divided into three distinct categories—*pop, country,* and *rhythm and blues* (aka "race music"). There were occasional crossovers from one musical area into another but, in general, the three areas were isolated.

Pop was the musical style that sold to adult listeners outside of the South. Pop records were usually ballads or novelty songs which featured a subdued beat and smooth singing. Many of the ballads were love songs. But unlike the sexual and emotional love in blues or gospel music, pop vocalists usually handled these feelings in a sentimental or melodramatic manner.

On the whole, rhythm and blues records had a far more direct approach to love and sex. This directness was driven home by a pounding, sensual dance beat. The rhythm and blues field consisted of black artists who recorded on small, independent labels (known as "indies"). The men who ran the "indies" believed that their records would sell only to black listeners. Occasionally, black artists would cross over into the white market. These artists usually sounded white and were, therefore, acceptable to listeners who would never consider purchasing a true rhythm and blues record.

Country and western music had its stronghold in the South and Southwest, though listeners in other locales were familiar with singing cowboys like Roy Rogers and Gene Autry from their films and television shows. Although country music was, in certain respects, close to rhythm and blues, it was far more palatable to the pop audience. Country artists such as Hank Williams sometimes crossed over into the pop market and their records sold well. Until recently, however, it was rare for a pop or rhythm and blues performer to cross over into country.

In the mid-fifties, two men had separate but related visions that helped to bring about the breakdown of these rigid divisions in popular music. Not coincidentally, both were astute businessmen. One was a Cleveland disk jockey named Alan Freed, and the other was the owner of a small Memphis-based record company named Sam Phillips. Both men had a genuine appreciation of rhythm and blues and both had a strong desire to make a lot of money. They both worked from the same premise: *If you could expand the audience for a particular kind of music, you could bring in more dollars.*

Alan Freed was a classical disk jockey in Cleveland until a record store owner made him aware of the growing demand by white teenagers for rhythm and blues records. Soon, Freed started playing rhythm and blues on a show he called "The Moondog Rock 'n' Roll House Party."

The expression "rock 'n' roll" was originally a black term for sex. By using this term to describe familiar rhythm and blues material, Freed helped give his young white audience the sense that this was a new music that had been created just for them. But as Bobby Robinson points out, "A lot of people who weren't aware of rhythm and blues thought Alan Freed invented this music, but that just isn't so. What he did was to introduce black music to the mass white audience and give it a new name."

Alan Freed—introduced
black music to young,
white listeners.

Rhythm and blues singer Screamin' Jay Hawkins
is a survivor of the fifties who opened for the Rolling
Stones during their 1982 American tour. Screamin'
Jay was in Cleveland when Alan Freed built his repu-
tation. He also remembers how rough things were for
R&B performers in those days.

The early fifties was a time when there was still a great
deal of prejudice in the world. I remember that Roy
Hamilton (a black singer) had a white piano player. If he
went past the Mason-Dixon Line, anywhere down
South, they would draw the curtain between Roy and
the piano player—who had to play from behind the curtain. In the deep South . . . they didn't permit blacks and
whites on the stage together at the same time. They had
one show for the blacks and one show for the whites.
Both shows would be curtained off. If you had a group
that was mixed, they wanted the black singers separated
from the white singers so the audience would not see
whites on the same stage with blacks. These were the

conditions in the late forties and early fifties. Alan Freed was a big reason for changing all that. The music that Alan Freed called rock 'n' roll was originally called blues. At one point, it became rhythm and blues. Then, Alan Freed changed its name to rock 'n' roll.

Alan Freed called people like Chuck Berry, Bo Diddley, Fats Domino, and myself rock 'n' rollers; our music is rhythm and blues, not rock 'n' roll. Freed just coined the term to sell the music to a bigger audience. He called it "the big beat." At his shows, Freed had a twenty-three-piece orchestra with two drummers. It was the loudest sound anyone ever heard before punk rock came along.

Screamin' Jay recalls that some black performers resented Freed's style at first. Ultimately, they realized that he was introducing black artists and their music to thousands of new listeners.

Before Alan Freed, Cleveland only had one radio station that catered to black music. One day, on a white radio station, a guy came on that sounded black. It was actually Alan Freed, but at that time he was calling himself Moondog. He had a wolf sound that he began his shows with. After the wolf, there would be a few bars of black music and then his voice would come in: "Hi, this is Moondog playing you some more of those snappy sounds that I have coined rock 'n' roll."

For a while, we were kind of upset about there being a black dude on a white radio station playing black music. But after black people saw his first show, we were quite pleased. Freed featured black music and black music only. In those days you could count everybody in show business that was black on your fingers. So naturally, we were happy to see that our music was finally getting played on a white radio station. You can't overestimate how much Alan Freed helped black artists.

At first, as Screamin' Jay notes, the term rock 'n' roll was just a new name for rhythm and blues. But it was a name that made white kids feel that they had their own music. This simple name change resulted in a boom in record sales.

Before long, record producers and songwriters started gearing their music for this new audience. Many rock 'n' roll records were nothing more than watered-down imitations of rhythm and blues. Pat Boone, for example, made a fortune recording lame versions of songs by Little Richard and Fats Domino. But soon, original artists like Chuck Berry were combining the feel of rhythm and blues with lyrics that were aimed at white teenagers.

Doc Pomus remembers when he first started writing songs that were specifically tailored for this new market.

> The first record that I ever heard that was really geared to young people was Frankie Lymon and the Teenagers' "Why Do Fools Fall In Love?" I couldn't relate to it at all until a few years later. . . . At that time, we were told that adults weren't buying records anymore, so try to gear the stuff for young people.

Before the mid-fifties, anyone who did not choose to hear rhythm and blues could easily avoid it. This stuff was *race music,* after all, and how many white people really cared about what was going on in the black ghettos? Then, white kids by the millions started buying these records, and it struck a chord of fear in many corners.

Paul Sherman is a disk jockey who often filled in for Alan Freed during his years at New York radio

station WINS. To this day, he cannot see why so many
parents were concerned about their children listening
to rhythm and blues–based music.

> I always thought that it was good for kids to have their
> own music, and I know that Alan felt the same way too. I
> never could understand why so many parents found
> rock 'n' roll objectionable. Alan never encouraged kids
> to go against their parents. But he did feel that it was
> important for young people to be independent. He
> couldn't see anything wrong with teenagers having their
> own music and their own styles. He talked about these
> things a great deal on his show. It's true that he made a
> lot of money from the business of rock 'n' roll, but he
> genuinely loved the music. . . .
>
> Alan felt that the beat was the main thing that attracted
> kids to rock 'n' roll. He felt that the *big beat* could never
> be big enough. He used to bang on a phone book over
> the air just to make sure that listeners could hear the
> beat.

The same beat that was so attractive to kids
created a response of racism in some adults. Wasn't
this a jungle beat? The sound of a primitive people?
These anti-black attitudes were most visible in the
South, where a number of violent incidents occurred.

One of the most disturbing of these took place in
Birmingham, Alabama, during a Nat "King" Cole
concert in 1956. This was ironic, since Cole was one of
the few black singers whose records were popular
among white adult listeners. Writer Nat Hentoff described this violent racial incident in the British music
publication *New Musical Express:*

> One of the world's most talented and respected singing
> stars, Nat "King" Cole, was the victim of a vicious attack

by a gang of six men at Birmingham, during his performance at a concert on Tuesday.

His assailants rushed down the aisles during his second number and clambered over the footlights. They knocked Nat down with such force that he hit his head and back on the piano stool, and they then dragged him into the auditorium.

Police rushed from the wings and were just in time to prevent the singer from being badly beaten up. They arrested six men, one of whom is a director of the White Citizen's Council—a group which has been [trying] to boycott "bop and Negro music" and are supporters of segregation of white and [black] people. The audience—numbering over 3,000—was all white.

Most of the attempts to suppress rhythm and blues and rock 'n' roll were not so directly violent. There were denouncements of the music in newspapers and record-smashing contests sponsored by radio stations. But on other occasions, things got out of hand.

In 1958, at one of Alan Freed's rock 'n' roll shows in Boston, police provoked the young audience by turning up the house lights in the middle of the program. Freed made a comment and the crowd became aroused. Later that day, there were a few violent incidents near the theater. Police blamed Freed for the trouble. He was arrested and charged with inciting a riot.

In time, all the charges against Freed were dropped. But because of the incident, Freed changed radio stations and spent thousands of dollars in legal fees. Late the following year, Alan Freed became the major target and most tragic figure of the "payola" scandal.

Before 1960, it was more or less accepted practice for disk jockeys to receive favors in exchange for playing a particular record. In addition, some of the more successful disk jockeys owned part interests in some of the songs and records they were playing. Since Alan Freed was listed as a cowriter on songs like Chuck Berry's "Maybelline" and the Moonglows' "Sincerely," there was an obvious conflict of interest. How, one might rightfully ask, could a disk jockey resist the temptation to push a record he had a financial interest in harder than one in which he had no interest?

Alan Freed probably did take part in these questionable practices. But it is unlikely that he was any more guilty than other disk jockeys who were relatively unscathed by the "payola" scandal. The feeling among many educated observers who were there at the time is that Freed was made a scapegoat because he was the disk jockey who had introduced rhythm and blues—that dangerous, primitive music—to white kids.

Freed was fired from his job at WABC when he refused to sign a statement that he had never accepted favors for playing rercords. In 1962, he was found guilty of two counts of commercial bribery, fined three hundred dollars, and given a six-month suspended sentence. Two years later, he was found guilty of income tax evasion.

Though he was still a young man, Alan Freed was tragically close to the end. He was banned from radio, broke from paying massive legal fees, and physically ill. In 1965, at the age of forty-three, "the father of rock 'n' roll" passed away. Doc Pomus, who counted himself as one of Alan Freed's friends, still gets angry when he thinks about how unfairly Freed was treated.

> If Alan Freed did take payola, he took less than most of those other DJs. One night, after they railroaded him out of the music business, Alan walked into Al & Vic's— a music business hangout. He said to me, "Do you want to take a vacation? Here's the keys to my house in Palm Beach." That was all he had left in the world, but he really wanted me to stay there because that's the kind of person he was. I didn't go. But the point is, he really tried to help people. Considering the kind of trash that was out there at the time, Alan was guiltless. But they made him the brunt of it and he drank himself to death.

The second astute businessman who had a major impact on rhythm and blues in the fifties also started out as a disk jockey, though he did not come to the same kind of tragic end as Alan Freed. Sam Phillips is still alive and basking in the glory of being one of the people who was most responsible for bringing rhythm and blues out of the ghetto. It was Sam Phillips who had the vision that was to alter the course of American popular music.

"If I could only find me a white boy with a black sound," Phillips had said many times, "I could make a million dollars." Then one day, a young truck driver for the Crown Electric Company came into Sam Phillips's Memphis recording studio. The singer's name was Elvis Presley.

When Sam Phillips first opened his recording studio at 706 Union Avenue in 1950, he was working as an engineer at a local radio station. Phillips decided to supplement his income with a recording service. "We Record Anything—Anywhere—Anytime" adver-

Elvis with guitarist Scotty Moore—influenced every rock act for the next twenty-five years.

tised the Memphis Recording Service. Most of Phillips's early jobs were weddings, funerals, and people who walked in off the street—like Elvis Presley.

One Saturday afternoon in 1954, Elvis walked into the Union Street studio to cut a record as a birthday present for his mother. The songs he chose were not blues, but ballads sung in the crooning style of Dean Martin. Still, Phillips's secretary, Marion Keisker, thought that Elvis had a quality that her boss might be able to do something with.

At first, Sam Phillips was not overwhelmed by Elvis's sound. It is unlikely that he thought that this was the million-dollar singer he had been waiting for. Besides, Sam Phillips was doing okay with his little studio.

Not long after he went into business, Phillips was contacted by a number of independent record labels who were interested in recording the work of the many talented, but unknown, blues singers who lived in the Memphis area. The deal these record companies offered Phillips was simple: find and record local blues singers with commercial potential. If the independent labels liked the results, they would lease the masters and give Phillips a percentage of all record sales.

This arrangement, with labels like Chess in Chicago and Modern in Los Angeles, put Phillips in the unexpected position of engineering and supervising the first recordings of some of the most important bluesmen of our time. B.B. King, Howlin' Wolf, and Bobby "Blue" Bland were among those to launch successful recording careers at 706 Union Avenue. Not only that—a number of the things Phillips recorded became top-ten rhythm and blues hits. In fact, one of those songs, "Rocket 88" by a singer named Jackie Brenston, became a number-one hit. The session that had produced "Rocket 88" and several other hits was put together by a piano playing disk jockey named Ike Turner.

Phillips also had success with Rufus Thomas, who recorded "Bearcat," an answer song to Willie Mae Thornton's "Hound Dog"; and with a group of convicts from Memphis State Prison—the Prisonaires—who recorded "Just Walkin' in the Rain." But between the Prisonaires' hit in April 1953 and Elvis's first release, Phillips did not have a single record on the charts.

Perhaps it was this dry spell that caused Phillips to work with a young and not very impressive singer.

Rufus Thomas, one
of Sam Phillips's
early success stories.

Or maybe Phillips was taken by the way his secretary
went on about how good-looking and sexy Elvis was.
Sam Phillips had Elvis come to the studio several
times. The results weren't encouraging. Then he put
Elvis together with two young, ambitious musicians—
guitarist Scotty Moore and bass player Bill Black. The
three began to rehearse, and discovered that they all
had a similar feel for the blues. Then, on July 6, 1954,
Phillips hit on the sound he had been looking for.
Elvis described the events that led up to that night in
the British magazine, *Hit Parader.*

> Mr. Phillips said he'd coach me if I'd come over to the
> studio as often as I could. It must have been a year and a
> half before he gave me an actual session. At last he let
> me try a Western song—and it sounded terrible. But the
> second idea was the one that jelled.
>
> "You want to make some blues?" he suggested over the
> phone, knowing I'd be a sucker for that kind of jive. He

mentioned Big Boy Cruddup's name and maybe others too; I don't remember.

All I know is I hung up and ran fifteen blocks to Mr. Phillips's office before he'd gotten off the line. . . . We talked about the Cruddup records I knew—"Cool Disposition," "Rock Me Mamma," "Everything's All Right," and others. We finally settled for "That's All Right," one of my favorites. . . ."

On that hot summer night in 1954, musical history was made. Some say it was the night that rock 'n' roll was born. Others have noted that it forever dispelled the notion that rhythm and blues could not be handled by a white singer. But to guitarist Scotty Moore, the music that was made that night was no big deal. After all, he, Bill Black, and Elvis had been messing around with the blues for months. As Moore told writer Albert Goldman in the book *Elvis:*

> Elvis just started clowning. . . . I joined in, as soon as I found out what key we were in. Then, the control room doors opened, Sam was in there doin' somethin', and he came out and said: "What are y'all doin'?" Elvis said, "I don't know—just goofin' off!" Sam said, "Well, that sounds pretty good. Back up and see if you can figure out what you're doin', and let's put it on tape." So we kinda talked it over and figured out a little bit what we were doin'. We ran it again, and of course, Sam is listenin'. 'Bout the third or fourth time through we just cut it—and that was that! It was basically a rhythm record. It wasn't any great thing. It wasn't Sam tellin' him what to do. Elvis was joking around just doing what come naturally, what he felt.

As far as Sam Phillips was concerned, this was it. He had found the sound he had been after all this time. Phillips was much more than another businessman who happened to be in the right place at the right time. He made a significant contribution to both that historic session and the Presley sound. As Albert Goldman notes:

> Sam Phillips skillfully seconded [Elvis's] inspired interpretation [of the blues] by enhancing the high ecstatic voice with a subtle aura of quavering echo. It's worth noting that this was the first time Phillips ever employed this effect in recording a white singer. It was a stroke of genius—perhaps the most brilliant inspiration of this famous producer's career. Indeed, when you weigh the forces that contributed to Elvis Presley's breakthrough, Phillips's claim to importance appears completely justified. Not only did he give Elvis the right steer in directing him away from . . . [mushy] ballads to the currently fashionable R&B material, but he attached to his new star's raw and untrained voice the electronic [element] that masked his vocal faults while it transformed . . . his vocal quality into the now legendary Presley sound.

Phillips also deserves credit for convincing local disk jockeys to play this revolutionary record. Remember, Memphis was part of the South, where there was still a strict social and musical segregation. Who would play this kind of a record? Black disk jockeys wouldn't be interested in a white blues singer. At the same time, country disk jockeys would find the sound too black for their listeners.

Through his persistence, Sam was able to convince a local disk jockey named Dewey Phillips (no relation) to play "That's All Right Mamma" on his show. Listener response was unprecedented. This record and its follow-ups on the Sun label were all hits in the South.

Sam Phillips was a shrewd businessman as well as a talented producer. He knew that some people would object to this "white boy who stole the blues." To protect his investment, Phillips backed up each rhythm and blues record Elvis recorded with a country song. That way, if disk jockeys didn't want to play the blues side, Sam would just tell them to "flip it over."

Elvis's singing on the country sides was good, though not exceptional. On the blues sides, however, you can hear him inventing a kind of music that nobody had ever heard before. Here was a new kind of blues singer with a new approach to the music.

Instead of crying or shouting the blues, Elvis sang in a way that suggested a man seeking independence and good times. Charlie Gillett describes Elvis's revolutionary interpretation of the blues as one which suggests "a young white man celebrating his freedom, ready to do anything, go anywhere, pausing long enough for apologies and even regrets, but then hustling on toward the new. . . ."

Even if Elvis wasn't the greatest rhythm and blues singer of his era, he had provided the young white audience something that his black forerunners could not: *He was white and sexy.* It was only a matter of time until he would outgrow Phillips's small record company. In late 1955, Elvis signed with RCA for the then astounding sum of fifty thousand dollars. Within a few months, he became the biggest star in popular music history. Soon, everyone in the music business was looking for *the next Elvis.*

Not surprisingly, Sam Phillips came up with better white rhythm and blues singers than anyone else. Carl Perkins, a skilled guitarist and songwriter, had a hit with "Blue Suede Shoes" immediately after Elvis left Sun. Unfortunately, for Phillips and Perkins, Elvis recorded the song on his first RCA album, and his version became far more popular than the original.

Phillips also discovered Jerry Lee Lewis—a frantic piano-playing singer who reminded people of a white Little Richard. Lewis had smash hits with "Whole Lotta Shakin' Goin' On" and "Great Balls of Fire." But his career took a dramatic downturn because of the bad publicity he received after he married his teenage cousin.

Other record labels tried to find their own answers to Elvis. Capitol Records came close with Gene Vincent, who scored a big hit with "Be-Bop-a-Lula." Other companies were content with pretty boys who simply looked like Elvis. Singing ability was definitely secondary. This group of singers are remembered as the *teen idols*. These included Ricky Nelson—already a household name from his work on the popular TV show "Ozzie and Harriet"—Frankie Avalon, and Fabian.

Most of these teen idols faded into obscurity during the next few years. Elvis himself concentrated on rock 'n' roll for only a few more years. His manager, Colonel Tom Parker, was far more interested in the movies. That was a logical step. After all, these crazed kids were bound to outgrow Elvis and even rock 'n' roll itself. It seemed like good business sense to make Elvis the property of all Americans, not just a bunch of screaming teenagers.

So much has been said about Elvis over the years. Author Greil Marcus once called him "the supreme figure in American life." John Lennon, on the other hand, in commenting upon Elvis's death in 1977, said: "Elvis died the day he went into the army." What Lennon probably meant was that Elvis had long ago stopped being important to the development of rhythm and blues and rock 'n' roll. Yet, as Albert Goldman notes, the explosion Elvis caused between 1954 and 1957 is still being felt.

> Elvis's genius lay in combining the movie myth of the menacing teenager with rock 'n' roll music so as to create a whole new performance idiom appropriate to that wild new form of entertainment, the rock concert. Out of his threatening poses, frenzied gyrations and spontaneous psychodrama sprang the whole tradition of hard rock.

> Overnight, the basic image for a hot young singer became a crazy-looking boy with a guitar in his hand cutting up all over a stage. So profound and pervasive is this image today that we can't imagine a rock singer under any other aspect. Consequently, you could say that Elvis's influence as a stage performer far surpassed his effect as a recording star. . . . Every real rock act that followed him for the next twenty-five years derived from his stage rhetoric.

It may not be a pretty thought, but there is little doubt that Elvis's importance in the history of rhythm and blues and rock 'n' roll has as much to do with the fact that he was white as it does with his actual musical talent. Still, Elvis was much more than an imitator. Though he owed a great debt to black blues singers, the man definitely had his own sound. He was certainly a better singer and greater innovator than, say, Arthur Cruddup, writer of Elvis's first Sun hit. But many of Elvis's remakes of rhythm and blues hits by

Jerry Lee Lewis, Carl Perkins, Johnny Cash, Roy Orbison—all protegees of Sam Phillips.

people like Little Richard, Ray Charles, and Lloyd
Price don't approach the excitement of the originals.
Still, no black artist of that era could ever have
matched Elvis's success.

When a white teenager listened to Elvis, the question wasn't so much one of sound as of image. Here
was someone free and rebellious—someone whom a
young white boy could imitate, and a young white girl
could scream over.

As John Lennon observed, Elvis Presley only
made consistently great rock 'n' roll records for two
or three years. After that, he turned his attentions to
movie-making and other light but lucrative forms of
entertainment. His manager, Colonel Tom Parker,
thought that's where the money was, and maybe he
was right.

I think there is somewhat of a tendency to over-
rate Elvis's music because his total impact was so
great. Still, in some of the early RCA cuts, you can
hear a musical form that, while derived from rhythm
and blues, has an originality all its own. "Don't Be
Cruel" is one Presley song that fits this description.
But even here, there is controversy.

Otis Blackwell is the New York–based songwriter
who wrote "Don't Be Cruel" for Presley. A few years
ago, Gary Giddens, a respected jazz critic, wrote an
article for the *Village Voice,* which stated that Elvis had
borrowed much of his singing style from Blackwell.
But Doc Pomus—an old friend of Blackwell's—claims
that this was a story he planted to help a buddy
through a rough time.

Back in the mid-fifties, before Doc and his
songwriting partner, Mort Schuman, had many hit

songwriting credits, Otis had helped them out. Now Doc was returning the favor.

Otis and I grew up together in Brooklyn. We interchanged gigs, split our money. After Otis started making it, he connected me with a guy named Paul Chase—the professional manager of Hill and Range Music. Chase was a musical genius when it came to understanding songs. He was one of the few guys in that end of the business that I respected. Otis convinced the guy to listen to us. Chase offered us jobs as staff writers. I got two hundred dollars a week as advance on royalties. I had a pregnant wife at the time, and had not yet proven that I could write rock and roll hits, so I was always very thankful to Otis.

Years went by. Otis was having problems. His money was held up in litigation and he was drinking. By then, I was making money, leading a kind of structured life. So I wanted to help Otis out. I tried to get him to work and help him put bands together, but nothing would happen. It seemed as if Otis would always fall apart at the last minute.

One night, I went to the Other End [a well-known Greenwich Village club]. Billy Swan [a highly regarded R&B singer] was there and I asked him to phone Otis and invite him to sing. The next night Otis sang and brought down the house.

After the show, Gary Giddens comes over and says: "Wow, he sings just like Presley." Otis does sound like Elvis on certain kinds of songs, but Elvis was such a great singer in his own right. I'm sure he listened to Otis on the demos, but he always put a lot of his own thing into it. Anyway, I told Giddens that Elvis was greatly influenced by Otis, but I really don't know if that's true or not. Then he wrote this tremendous story about Otis in the *Voice* and the word got out that Otis was Elvis's big influence.

The frequent confusion between myth and reality doesn't make it any easier to answer the question we started out with: *Whatever happened to the rhythm and blues of the fifties?* Some of that era's most important heroes are dead or out of the business. Others are working the oldies circuit as a way of making some extra bucks and keeping their hand in show business. A few, like Gary Bonds, have reached new peaks in the eighties. Still others who started back then are working in much the same way they always worked.

Doc Pomus is still writing songs, Bobby Robinson is still producing records, and Screamin' Jay Hawkins is still working and trying to keep one step ahead of a treacherous business.

In thinking about the essential qualities of rhythm and blues in the fifties, we should never lose sight that it was, at its core, a good-humored music for dancing and having fun. Screamin' Jay Hawkins always understood the humorous side of rhythm and blues. In fact, he was the first to combine humor with a touch of voodo and horror. After he recorded "I Put A Spell On You," Screamin' Jay wanted to do something dramatic to get the song's message across.

> I bought a coffin and put it into the act. . . . I would open my show by coming out of the coffin screaming. Instead of just hearing the record as it was on the radio, people also saw a show. That way, if the music didn't sound exactly perfect, people could still enjoy a good show. . . .
>
> Now I am doing more or less like a Fats Domino type of act. I am on the piano more. But every once in a while

Screamin' Jay Hawkins—"On Halloween, they always know who to call."

I'll get up and start leaping and screaming and acting like a maniac and going into my witch doctor routine. I have apparatus where fire comes from my fingertips, I have hands that will crawl across the stage my themselves, I have teeth that chatter, I have a witch doctor stick called Henry, and I have a flash act which blows the whole place up with smoke. After the smoke clears, I am gone. After all these years, the whole vibe of the act is still grounded in that one song—"I Put A Spell On You."

Screamin' Jay becomes animated when he talks about all the people who have recorded his songs and those who have tried to copy his performance style over the years (the list includes everyone from the

Funkadelics to Creedence Clearwater Revival to Donny and Marie Osmond). Like all songwriters, Jay is pleased when others record his tunes, but he feels sorry for anyone who has to copy another's style. When you ask him what happened to that wonderful spirit of fifties rhythm and blues, Jay's answer is curt, but to the point:

> A lot of the stuff you hear today sounds like its only purpose is to make a dollar. I've started to close my ears to most of that music, because too much of it is missing the single most important ingredient that was behind the rhythm and blues of years gone by—*real emotion.*

## FIFTIES SELECTED DISCOGRAPHY

### CHUCK BERRY
Concerto in B Goode . . . . . . . . . . . . . . . . . . . . . . . . . . . . . Mercury
Golden Decade . . . . . . . . . . . . . . . . . . . . . . . . . . . . . . . . . . . Chess
Greatest Hits . . . . . . . . . . . . . . . . . . . . . . . . . . . . . . . . . . . . Chess
St. Louis to Liverpool . . . . . . . . . . . . . . . . . . . . . . . . . . . . Chess

### THE CLEFTONES
"Can't We Be Sweethearts" (Single) . . . . . . . . . . . . . . . . . . Gee
"Heart and Soul" (Single) . . . . . . . . . . . . . . . . . . . . . . . . . . Gee
"Little Girl of Mine" (Single) . . . . . . . . . . . . . . . . . . . . . . . . Gee

### THE COASTERS
Greatest Hits . . . . . . . . . . . . . . . . . . . . . . . . . . . . . . . . . . . . . Atco

### THE DEL VIKINGS
"Come Go with Me" (Single) . . . . . . . . . . . . . . . . . . . . . . . . Dot
"Whispering Bells" (Single) . . . . . . . . . . . . . . . . . . . . . . . . . Dot

### BO DIDDLEY
Bo Diddley . . . . . . . . . . . . . . . . . . . . . . . . . . . . . . . . . . . Checker

## FATS DOMINO
Fats Is Back............................ Warner Brothers
Million Sellers By Fats .......................... Imperial

## FIVE SATINS
"In the Still of the Night" (Single).................. Ember
"To the Aisle" (Single) ........................... Ember

## BILL HALEY AND THE COMETS
Rock Around the Clock............................ Decca

## THE HARPTONES
"Life Is But a Dream" (Single) ................... Paradise

## SCREAMIN' JAY HAWKINS
I Put A Spell On You................................ Epic
What That Is.................................... Phillips

## BUDDY HOLLY
The Buddy Holly Story ............................ Coral
Reminiscing....................................... Coral

## JERRY LEE LEWIS
The Golden Hits of Jerry Lee Lewis................... Smash
The Greatest Live Show on Earth .................... Smash
Original Golden Hits—Volumes I and II................. Sun

## FRANKIE LYMON
"The ABC's of Love" (Single) ........................ Gee
"Goody Goody" (Single) ............................. Gee
"I Promise to Remember" (Single)..................... Gee
"I Want You to Be My Girl" (Single) .................. Gee
"Why Do Fools Fall In Love?" (Single)................. Gee

## CARL PERKINS
"Blue Suede Shoes" (Single)......................... Sun
Old Blue Suede Shoes Is Back ................... Columbia

## THE PLATTERS
Double Gold Platters............................ Musicor
Encore of Golden Hits .......................... Mercury
More Encore of Golden Hits ...................... Mercury
New Golden Hits of the Platters.................... Musicor
Remember When ............................... Mercury
The Platters—Volumes I and II .................... Mercury

## ELVIS PRESLEY
Elvis's Golden Records—Volumes I, II, III, and IV .... RCA Victor
The Sun Sessions .............................. RCA VIctor
Elvis's 50 Worldwide Gold Award Hits—Volumes I and II
                                              RCA Victor

## THE PRISONAIRES
Five Beats Behind Bars...................... Charly (British)

## RUFUS THOMAS
Rufus Thomas ................................... Atlantic

## GENE VINCENT
"Be-Bop-a-Lula" (Single) .......................... Capitol

# CHAPTER 6

# GIRL GROUPS

## The Sound of the Early Sixties

*I've always been able to deal with things in a spiritual way by translating pain into something beautiful. But sometimes when I play those oldies shows, I wonder just what it is I'm doing, what kind of a path am I following?*

—Arlene Smith

By the early sixties, many of the artists who had transformed rhythm and blues styles into rock 'n' roll had either moved on to other things, died, or had lost their popularity. Elvis was out of the army, but had faded as a teen idol and a musical force. Little Richard was off preaching somewhere. Chuck Berry was having legal problems. Buddy Holly had been killed in a plane crash. Jerry Lee Lewis was banned from many radio stations because he had married his teenage cousin. Fats Domino simply wasn't turning out hits the way he used to. Most of the one-shot vocal groups from the fifties were long out of the music business.

In spite of these heavy losses, however, rhythm and blues was alive and well, but its character was changing and so was its gender. Though the era's most dominating figure was a man—Phil Spector— the most important popular records of the early six-

The Ronettes,
the Shirelles,
the Crystals,
and the Chantels.

ties were made by female vocal groups—more commonly known as *girl groups*.

For some reason, there were only four hit singles by girl groups before 1958: "Down the Aisle Of Love," by the Quintones; "Mr. Lee," by The Bobettes; "Eddie My Love," by The Teen Queens; and "Maybe," by the Chantels. During the same period, there had been hundreds of hits by one-shot male groups. The main role of the female groups during those years was to back up male vocalists. But in the early sixties, this all began to change.

Since many of the great male performers had already done their best work, record producers were searching for a new sound. This was provided by the girl groups. Unlike the many male vocal groups who had forged their songs on street corners, the girl group sound was put together by sophisticated record producers who controlled every aspect of what was recorded.

The Chantels were the first girl group to place more than one hit on the charts. Though their lead singer, Arlene Smith, has often been called the greatest of the girl-group singers, the Chantels had reached their commercial peak several years before the girl group sound became a recognizable style. Yet the experiences of Arlene Smith and the Chantels captured the essence of what was going on—both in the studio and behind the scenes during the girl group era.

It's hard to understand why girl groups didn't make more records in the fifties. Perhaps group singing was more of a social thing for boys, an extension of hanging out. Still, everyone agreed that some of

the younger boy singers sounded like girls—Frankie
Lymon in particular. But unlike Frankie Lymon and
most other young male group singers, the Chantels
didn't learn to sing on the street, but in the choir of
their Catholic school. "One reason that the group had
such a pure sound," Arlene Smith recalls, "is that we
were all trained in the same kind of music—
Gregorian chant and a cappella. We all went to Saint
Anthony's Catholic school and were all trained by a
very talented nun . . . whose commitment to music
was based on purity of tone and diction. This is where
we got our shared musical foundation."

When Arlene Smith heard Frankie Lymon and
the Teenagers sing "Why Do Fools Fall In Love?" it
seemed to open up a whole world of new possibilities
for her. She decided to do something about it.

"I'm just about the same age as Frankie Lymon,"
she reasoned. "If he can make it, so can I." Since
Arlene had already written the songs and developed
an original musical concept, she felt confident in ap-
proaching Frankie Lymon's producer, Richard Bar-
rett, and asking him to give the group a chance to
record. The result was a string of hits that far sur-
passed any other all-female vocal group in the fifties.

The Chantels had proven that girl groups could
sell records. Soon, others would try to follow their
lead. But Arlene was unique among her peers. Unlike
most of the girl group lead singers who followed her,
Arlene had a vocal style that wasn't sexy or street
tough. Instead, it was pure and soulful. Though she
was very young, Arlene never did see herself as clay
to be molded by some older male producer. She may

have only been a teenager, but she had her own musical ideas.

> At the age of two, I was making up operas, without even knowing what an opera was. I was trying to express myself and entertain people even then. I always wanted to tell people about me. I wanted them to know me. When we started recording, I knew I had to give it as much energy as I could. When somebody played my record in their house, I wanted the message to still be there as strongly as I meant it. When you put your heart and soul into something, it is important to be believed.

Arlene never thought of singing as an easy road to fame and fortune. She used music as an extension of her feelings and an expression of what came naturally to her.

> My adolescent period was a time of emotion and mixed-up feelings. I had a really strong feeling of love. I didn't come out of a wealthy home. But it was a closely knit household. I never heard my father raise his voice and I was never disrespectful. I complained a lot because I thought they were strict, but I did what I thought I was supposed to do. God gave me two legs and I walked on them. God gave me a voice and I used it. I had no pretensions, and I guess I was pretty naive.

Perhaps it was that same naive quality that helped make Arlene's singing on songs like "Maybe," "I Love You So," and "He's Gone" so convincing. That idealized kind of love reflected the feelings of many young people at the time. Sounding naive may have sold records, but actually being naive wasn't very helpful to a fourteen-year-old girl trying to make it in a tough business.

Black teenage performers were particularly easy marks for ruthless businessmen. Arlene had a strong sense that some of the people she was dealing with were dishonest. But, as she recalls, there really wasn't very much she could do about it.

"I knew I was being had," she recalls, "but I was not allowed to say anything. I remember looking at some of the people who were handling our business and feeling that they were dishonest. But I didn't dare say anything about it because they were adults. It was a painful experience, trusting adults and finding out later that they were lying to you. The injustice of a lot of stuff that goes on in the music business still knocks me out. I would have been all right in the business, too, if they had left me alone to do my music and treated me more fairly."

Arlene shrugs her shoulders when she talks about how badly the Chantels were mismanaged. "We should all be independently wealthy women now," she says. "I remember getting fifteen dollars a week allowance when I had the hits. But I never received any record or songwriting royalties. I wrote 'Maybe' and 'He's Gone.' My name is on the label, but not on the contracts for royalty payments. Someone is still making a lot of money on me."

After the hits stopped coming and the Chantels discovered that they were not going to collect the money they had earned, there was a period of finger-pointing and in-fighting between Arlene and the rest of the group. Everyone thought that you could get rich off one hit record, and the Chantels had scored three hits. The bad feelings were too intense for the group to stay together, so they went their separate ways.

Now that the Chantels had split up, Arlene got the opportunity to work with Phil Spector—the man who had been so influential in shaping the girl group sound. But as we've seen, Arlene Smith wasn't the typical girl group singer. She felt strongly about her musical ideas and the message she wanted to get across. Apparently, this clashed with Spector's need to maintain complete control in the studio. Still, Arlene was happy that she finally had the chance to record as a solo artist.

> I was finally enjoying an independence that I never knew before. At last, I was doing something as Arlene Smith. Even if I never made a dollar, it was very important to me to get that kind of personal recognition. I was signed to Big Top and Phil Spector was my producer. I was in my glory with the big sessions we were doing. But things with Big Top never really materialized.
>
> Phil Spector's whole thing was big arrangements. He used every kind of drum, every kind of string, every kind of everything. But my kind of music does not require complicated arrangements. Instead of dealing with me as a unique voice, they would give me a piece of material that was written for somebody else and then expect me to make it sound like Arlene Smith. . . . They tried to mold me in the fashion of someone else, and that was a mistake.

Perhaps one of Arlene's problems was that she was too unique and unwilling to be molded by a producer—even one as skilled as Phil Spector. Most of the girl groups who followed the Chantels were, for the most part, pawns in some male producer's master plan. But ironically, the first girl group after the Chantels to have a series of hits recorded for one of the few record labels owned and operated by a woman.

The first successful releases on Florence Greenberg's Sceptor Records were by four teenage girls who called themselves the Shirelles. Their early singles, "Tonight's the Night" and "I Met Him on a Sunday," became the classic models for dozens of other female groups. Unlike Arlene Smith, who had a full, controlled voice, the Shirelles' lead singer, Shirley Alston, sounded raw and often cracked on her high notes. Still, her voice had a plaintive soulfulness and a youthful sensuality that was the model for most of the girl groups that became popular during the next few years.

The music of female vocal groups was built on a very crafty formula: 1) find a group with the right sound, 2) hire professional young songwriters like Carole King or Ellie Greewich to provide the right kind of tune, and 3) make the production big, but keep that dance beat pushing through. A number of producers used this formula with great success, but Phil Spector turned it into art.

In the early sixties, while still in his teens, Spector founded his own Philles record label. Though he wasn't successful with Arlene Smith at Big Top, he soon found other vehicles for his ideas. Spector's first group, the Crystals, were recorded in a style inspired by the Shirelles. As he continued to work with the group, Spector evolved his own recording style which he called "a wall of sound."

By using full orchestras and large rhythm sections, Spector added a majestic quality to the youthful yearnings expressed in the Crystals' songs. Simple an-

Carole King—one of the young songwriters who helped shape the girl-group sound.

thems of love like "Da Doo Ron Ron," and "Then He Kissed Me" were converted by Spector into experiences of high drama set to a pounding beat.

Spector used a similar style with his second group, the Ronettes. These girls had a tougher, less vulnerable image than most of their contemporaries. Their piled-up hair and streetwise look made their first song, "Be My Baby," seem as much of a challenge as an invitation. Their second hit, "Walking in the Rain," praised boys who were both strong and sensitive. These were the kinds of males who were the heroes of many girl group songs of that era—tough boys who knew how to be tender, secure boys who didn't need to act macho to win a girl's heart.

Though Spector was the most important girl group producer, there were a number of groups whose records were of comparable quality. The Marvelettes leaned more toward gospel music in songs like "Please Mr. Postman," and "Playboy," The Chiffons devised particularly unique background chants in their hits "He's So Fine," and "One Fine Day", while the Jaynettes captured the feeling of gossip being whispered in the shadows with their unusually haunting "Sally Go 'Round The Roses."

As with any form, female vocal group music also had its excesses. There was Rosie and the Originals, whose "Angel Baby" was one of the rawest and most out-of-tune records of its era, and the Shangri-Las with their melodramatic soap operas, "Leader Of The Pack" and "Remember (Walkin' in the Sand)."

On the whole, though, the music made by female vocal groups holds up extremely well today. Its immediate influence is apparent in the records of the Beatles, and its echoes still reverberate in the work of contemporary rock artists like Cyndi Lauper, the Go-Go's, and even Bruce Springsteen. But what of the great talents who originated the music?

Phil Spector has been in semiretirement since 1966. After an Ike and Tina Turner record that he produced called "River Deep, Mountain High" was not a big hit in America, Spector decided that the public did not deserve the benefits of his talents. In fact, the record was as good as Spector thought it was, even if it didn't make the top ten.

There have been many rumors about Phil Spector since his departure from the music business. He has, on occasiosn, come out of his self-imposed exile to do a project, including some work with the Beatles, John and Yoko, and the Ramones. But these records pale when compared to his triumphs with the Crystals, the Ronettes, and a male duo called the Righteous Brothers. His personal life—bizarre even by show business standards—has become a topic of almost as much fascination as his musical genius.

Interestingly, Spector married one of his discoveries, the former Veronica Bennett, lead singer of the Ronettes in the late sixties. In 1980, six years after divorcing her husband, Ronnie Spector began talking about what it was like living with Phil in the Beverly Hills mansion he had bought her was a wedding present. As she told *Rolling Stone*'s Kurt Loder:

> I *hated* living there. I felt like I was ninety years old. I was knitting rugs and doing paint-by-number pictures of *The Blue Boy.* I had absolutely no friends. No rock 'n' roll was played in the house. Sometimes at night, if I couldn't sleep, Phil would play Tony Bennett and Frank Sinatra—those kind of records put me to sleep. After a while I went *stir crazy.* I wasn't allowed to empty ashtrays. I couldn't go into the kitchen—that would mess up the cook's stuff . . . I couldn't wear a bikini in my own swimming pool—there was nobody there but me and Phil, but there were a lot of men servants. . . .

Now that she has broken ties with her dictatorial former producer/husband, Ronnie Spector has done better than most of the other girl group lead singers. She does work the occasional oldies show, but she also draws good crowds at some of the better rock clubs. Hit records continue to elude her, but at least she's gotten the chance to make records in the eighties—a precious opportunity that has been denied most of her contemporaries from the early sixties.

Arlene Smith's music career hasn't fared nearly so well as Ronnie Spector's. Every now and then, someone writes an article remembering her as one of the great voices of an era gone by. It has been a quarter of a century since Arlene's magnificent voice graced the top-forty charts. Nevertheless, she has lead a productive life and made valuable contributions in other arenas.

After her music career faded in the sixties, Arlene went to college to "try to better understand my adolescence so that I could deal with feeling like a has-been at twenty-two." In time, she graduated and then received her master's degree. Today, Arlene is a social worker who runs a day-care center in the South Bronx. The gratification she receives from this work is not all that different from singing.

"Working with kids in day-care centers does something good for my head," Arlene says. "It makes me feel important and it gives me an audience. They may just be little kids, but they're still an audience. . . . I've been doing this kind of work now for about twenty years and I find it very satisfying."

Arlene still sings on weekends, mostly at oldies shows. She loves music as much as she did when she was young, but sometimes finds it a bit strange to be singing the same songs now as she did when she was fourteen.

I have problems with personal appearances because the public thinks I'm something that I'm not. When the records came out, people thought that I sounded grown

Arlene Smith on her job at a day-care center in the South Bronx, New York.

up. Now, they think, "She must be at least seventy." In the concerts now, I am doing an imitation of myself. I am emulating fourteen- and fifteen-year-old emotions, though I have transcended that several times. I've always been able to deal with things in a spiritual way by translating pain into something beautiful. But sometimes when I play those oldies shows, I wonder just what it is I'm doing, what kind of a path am I following?

Looking back, Arlene has few regrets about her life. There is still some pain about not receiving the royalties she was entitled to—tens of thousands of dollars at least—far more than a social worker or an oldies performer can earn. Still, Arlene feels lucky to have found a fulfilling career and lucky to still be singing. She hasn't quite given up on making a major comeback. But this time, she vows that she will be at the helm, calling the shots.

> I have a different perspective now than I had when I was younger, even if I can't completely shed my past. . . . We once talked about re-forming the original Chantels group and working together again. But I realized that there was too much pain associated with my coming up, so I don't think we will ever work together again. A group needs to have a certain kind of personal and spiritual harmony. You can't really sing right if you don't have it. I realize now that I have to do my own thing. I am never again going to be told by anyone what I can and cannot do.

The hard personal struggles and the questionable business practices that affected the Chantels and their contemporaries cannot diminish the lasting appeal of female vocal group music. In fact, these issues have, to some extent, rekindled an interest in the style. The music these groups made holds up extremely well, but the form was commercially short-lived because audiences never were presented with the kind of strong image that superstars possess.

The Beatles, who borrowed extensively from the girl group sound, had several things going for them that their black, female counterparts did not: They had distinct personalities that somehow became incorporated into their music; they wrote many of their own songs; and they played their own instruments. Nevertheless, the best girl group music does not have to take a back seat to the early Beatles or to any other popular style. As writer Greil Marcus noted in *The Rolling Stone Illustrated History of Rock and Roll:*

[Girl group music contained] emotion of staggering intensity, unforgettable melodies, great humor, a good deal of rage, and a lot more struggle—the struggle, one might think, of the singer, a young girl, black as likely as not, against the domination of her white male producer. The relationship between singer and producer was dependent; almost none of the great singers of female group rock achieved even minimal success outside the direction of the producer originally responsible for her.

Marcus might also have added that most of the producers who grew rich off this sound stopped creating hits soon after they split with their female vocal groups.

## GIRL GROUP SELECTED DISCOGRAPHY

### THE BOBETTES
"Mr. Lee" (Single). . . . . . . . . . . . . . . . . . . . . . . . . . . . . . . . Atlantic

### THE CHANTELS
"I Love You So" (Single). . . . . . . . . . . . . . . . . . . . . . . . . . . End
"Look In My Eyes" (Single) . . . . . . . . . . . . . . . . . . . . . . . . End
"Maybe" (Single) . . . . . . . . . . . . . . . . . . . . . . . . . . . . . . . . End

### THE CHIFFONS
The Chiffons. . . . . . . . . . . . . . . . . . . . . . . . . . . . . . . . . . . . Laurie
Everything You Always Wanted. . . . . . . . . . . . . . . . . . . . . . Laurie
One Fine Day. . . . . . . . . . . . . . . . . . . . . . . . . . . . . . . . . . . . Laurie
Sweet Talking Guy . . . . . . . . . . . . . . . . . . . . . . . . . . . . . . . Laurie

### THE CRYSTALS
He's a Rebel. . . . . . . . . . . . . . . . . . . . . . . . . . . . . . . . . . . . Philles
Greatest Hits. . . . . . . . . . . . . . . . . . . . . . . . . . . . . . . . . . . . Philles
Wall of Sound Volume III. . . . . . . . . . . . . . . . . . . . . . Phil Spector

### THE JAYNETTES
"Sally Go 'Round the Roses" (Single). . . . . . . . . . . . . . . . . Tuff

## THE MARVELETTES
Anthology . . . . . . . . . . . . . . . . . . . . . . . . . . . . . . . . . . . . . . . . . . . . . . Motown
Best of the Marvelettes . . . . . . . . . . . . . . . . . . . . . . . . . . . . Motown
Greatest Hits. . . . . . . . . . . . . . . . . . . . . . . . . . . . . . . . . . . . . . . . . Motown
Playboy. . . . . . . . . . . . . . . . . . . . . . . . . . . . . . . . . . . . . . . . . . . . . . Motown
Please Mr. Postman . . . . . . . . . . . . . . . . . . . . . . . . . . . . . . . Motown
Return of the Marvelettes. . . . . . . . . . . . . . . . . . . . . . . . . . Motown

## QUINTONES
"Down the Aisle of Love" (Single) . . . . . . . . . . . . . . . . . . . Hunt

## ROSIE AND THE ORIGINALS
"Angel Baby" (Single) . . . . . . . . . . . . . . . . . . . . . . . . . . . . . . . Hunt

## THE RONETTES
Fabulous Ronettes . . . . . . . . . . . . . . . . . . . . . . . . . . . . . . . . . . . Philles
The Ronettes . . . . . . . . . . . . . . . . . . . . . . . . . . . . . . . . . . . . . . . Colpix
Today's Hits. . . . . . . . . . . . . . . . . . . . . . . . . . . . . . . . . . . . . . . . . Philles

## THE SHANGRI-LAS
Golden Hits. . . . . . . . . . . . . . . . . . . . . . . . . . . . . . . . . . . . . . . . Mercury
I Can Never Go Home . . . . . . . . . . . . . . . . . . . . . . . . . . . Red Bird
Leader of the Pack. . . . . . . . . . . . . . . . . . . . . . . . . . . . . . . . Red Bird
Shangri-Las '65 . . . . . . . . . . . . . . . . . . . . . . . . . . . . . . . . . . . Red Bird

## THE SHIRELLES
Baby It's You. . . . . . . . . . . . . . . . . . . . . . . . . . . . . . . . . . . . . . . Sceptor
Foolish Little Girl . . . . . . . . . . . . . . . . . . . . . . . . . . . . . . . . . . Sceptor
Greatest Hits—Volumes I and II . . . . . . . . . . . . . . . . . . . . Sceptor
Remember When—Volumes I and II. . . . . . . . . . . . . . . . . Sceptor
Shirelles Sing the Golden Oldies . . . . . . . . . . . . . . . . . . . . Sceptor
Tonight's the Night. . . . . . . . . . . . . . . . . . . . . . . . . . . . . . . . . Sceptor
The Shirelles Sing Their Best . . . . . . . . . . . . . . . . . . . . Springboard
The Very Best of the Shirelles . . . . . . . . . . . . . . . . . . . . . . . . . UA

## THE TEEN QUEENS
"Eddie My Love" (Single) . . . . . . . . . . . . . . . . . . . . . . . . . . . RMP

# CHAPTER 7

# MOTOWN

## Rhythm and Blues Becomes "The Sound of Young America"

*Just give me money, that's what I want.*

—"Money" by Berry Gordy

In the early sixties, an independently owned Detroit record company brought about a revolution in rhythm and blues. That company's name is Motown —short for motor-town. More than two decades after it almost completely dominated popular music, the commercial and artistic achievements of Motown records and its president, Berry Gordy, are still unmatched. Even Phil Spector, the self-proclaimed Babe Ruth of popular music, freely acknowledges that Gordy and his staff of talented producers were the first to make unadulterated rhythm and blues palatable to millions of white listeners.

By 1965, Motown's producers had succeeded in blending older rhythm and blues and gospel styles with sophisticated arrangements and recording techniques into what Berry Gordy called *"the sound of young America."* A typical mid-sixties Motown hit was characterized by a strong beat, gospel background singing, and lush musical arrangements behind a distinctive rhythm and blues voice. Although some of these records were slick and overproduced, many of Motown's hits are still unsurpassed examples of popular music at its best.

Almost as legendary as the music itself is the rise of Berry Gordy from a Detroit automobile assembly line to the head of one of America's richest black-owned corporations. Success did not come quickly to Gordy. He had tried his hand at boxing, and at operating a record store that specialized in jazz. Then, after his record store went bankrupt, Gordy decided to redirect his love of music and his business ambitions into songwriting. His earliest attempts did not materialize. But soon, together with his sister Gwen, Berry wrote "Reet Petite," "Lonely Teardrops," "To Be Loved," and several other hit records for Jackie Wilson. In spite of his growing catologue of hit tunes, though, Gordy was broke until he wrote a song called "Money." As he told *Record World:*

> . . . I didn't actually make any money from the songs I was writing, because by the time I got my royalties, I owed everybody in town, especially my family. I was broke up until the time I wrote "Money," even though I had many hits. . . . I was sort of embarrassed, and my family was somewhat embarrassed, because when people asked me what I did for a living, I would say, "I write songs." Their friends had sons and daughters that were becoming doctors, lawyers, the things that had great status, and my mother and father were always embarrassed when I told their friends that I wrote songs. "I know," they'd say, "but what do you do for a living?" I'd say again, "I write songs," and they'd ask if I'd made any money yet. I'd say, "No, not yet, but I will."

The Temptations, Mary Wells,
Martha and the Vandellas,
Smokey and the Miracles.

Jackie Wilson—
Berry Gordy penned
a number of this
great singer's hits.

In spite of his financial problems, Gordy was developing a local reputation as a talented songwriter and record producer. He had produced a number of his songs and leased them to other labels for a percentage of sales. Here again, Gordy was disappointed to discover that his records rarely received the kind of promotion he felt they warranted. And even when his records sold, he almost never collected all the royalties he had coming.

At this point, Berry Gordy decided to start his own record label. This daring step—and Motown's eventual success—made Gordy a legend. His rise from automobile assembly-line worker to entertainment-business tycoon looked like the fulfillment of the American Dream. Gordy's phenomenal rise to power was particularly notable because the hero was black.

By the early sixties, blacks had become important contributors in many sections of the entertainment field. There were black athletes in all major sports and successful black singers and musicians in jazz and popular music. But there were very few black people who wielded power as either owners or executives of record companies.

It should be stressed that while Berry Gordy was to become the most visible and successful black record company owner in music history, he was not the first. That distinction went to Bobby Robinson, who launched his first label in 1953. Robinson remembers that after several of Gordy's independent productions on other labels proved unprofitable, he asked the more experienced man for advice.

> Berry Gordy came to me before he started his label and I told him a lot of things. He had some of his records distributed by other companies and was disillusioned by the results. So he decided to take a shot at it himself. He came to me and asked: "What are the pitfalls, what do I look for?" So I told him the key markets to break a record and all the other things.

Though Bobby Robinson taught Gordy something about the ins and outs of owning a record company, it was another man named Robinson who provided much of the musical inspiration that helped launch Motown. Bobby reflects on his namesake's major contributions to Motown's success:

> As far as I'm concerned, Smokey Robinson has not been given enough credit in Berry Gordy and Motown's suc-

cess. If Berry Gordy hadn't met up with Smokey Robinson, the Motown story might have been a lot different. The way I see it, Smokey Robinson was the farmer who grew the great, beautiful apples. Berry Gordy was the trucker who took those apples to market. Without Smokey growing those apples, Berry would have had an empty truck.

Here's what it comes down to: Smokey Robinson was the key creator and the basic musical influence at Motown. He created the sound, not only with his own group, but with the Temptations, Mary Wells, Marvin Gaye, the Marvelettes, and others. Maybe as the trucker who understood the market place, Berry Gordy said: "Grow me some different kind of apples so I can market them better." But Smokey Robinson was the first major creative source at Motown. When you start a new enterprise, it's essential to have such a great creative talent on your side right away.

William "Smokey" Robinson provided Motown with its first top-ten hit—"Shop Around" by the Miracles in 1960. Smokey was the group's lead singer, as well as its writer and producer. He had a smooth, high-pitched voice that was influenced by Sam Cooke. A dynamic live performer, Robinson was adept at singing both exciting fast-dance numbers like "Mickey's Monkey" and "Going to a Go Go," and romantic, slow ballads like "You've Really Got a Hold on Me" and "The Tracks of my Tears."

Smokey was much more than the main cog in Motown's first hit group. In addition to writing and producing for other Motown stars, he and other members of the Miracles helped bring people like Diana Ross and Stevie Wonder to the label. Yet in spite of Smokey Robinson's enormous contributions, it was Berry Gordy who first envisioned the Motown sound that would dominate the charts for much of

Smokey Robinson—
the key creator of the
early Motown sound.

the sixties. The Miracles had been turned down by a number of record companies, but Gordy heard potential in both the group and their lead singer's songwriting talents. As Smokey was to recall years later:

> I must have [played him] . . . sixty-eight of my songs. And on every one I'd say, "What's wrong with this one?" and he'd say, "Well, you left off this or you didn't complete your idea on that," which really started me to think about songs and what they were. Gordy, man, that cat more than anyone else helped me get my things together.

In time, Smokey Robinson was to gain recognition as one of the finest popular songwriters ever. The

Beatles and the Rolling Stones recorded many of Smokey's tunes, and Bob Dylan once referred to him as "my favorite poet." Smokey's lyrical skills are undeniable, as Charlie Gillett notes in *The Sound of the City:*

> Robinson had an unusual consistency in the kind of songs he wrote, regularly hinging them on some curious contradiction in love, whose mystery provided the songs with a distinctive air of innocence, wonder, and discovery: "I got sunshine on a cloudy day" ("My Girl"); "Honey, you do me wrong but I still think about you" ("Ain't That Peculiar"); "People say I'm the life of the party 'cause I tell a joke or two. Although I may be laughing loud and hearty, deep inside I'm blue" ("The Tracks of my Tears").

Robinson's musical and lyrical abilities flourished under Berry Gordy's tutelage. The musical direction that Gordy helped Smokey Robinson achieve was somewhat comparable to that which Sam Phillips had forged with Elvis Presley a few years earlier. Phillips had managed to find a white performer who could adapt the black feel and sell millions of records. Now Gordy wanted to achieve a similar effect with black artists.

Somehow, Berry Gordy was determined to make pure rhythm and blues records that were softened just enough to appeal to young white listeners. This he managed to do. But amazingly, on his best records, Gordy retained enough authenticity to attract black listeners as well. Here's how Bobby Robinson describes this amalgam of rhythm and blues and pop that Motown came up with:

> Berry Gordy took the black sound and, without changing it too much, made it accessible to whites. While he

did dilute the authentic sound a little bit, he added an excitement, a beat, and a drive that young listeners couldn't resist. The religious fervor and the real blues wails were muted to a degree. But Gordy made up for it with a drive and a beat that gave Motown records an across-the-board appeal.

Some of Motown's most appealing and least diluted early records were sung by Marvin Gaye. Gaye had previously worked with the Moonglows—a vocal group that had achieved some success in the fifties. Originally employed as a session drummer by Gordy, Marvin Gaye's early records like "Can I Get a Witness" and "Pride and Joy" combined the music and language of the black church with the dance beat of rhythm and blues. Gaye's gospel influence was not surprising, since he began singing in his minister father's Washington, D.C., church.

The early Marvin Gaye records had a stomping drum beat and bass line, which was reinforced with gospel hand clapping and tambourines. These became trademarks on the early Motown sound, a sound that Gordy described as "rats, roaches, talent, guts, and love, because that's what it was in those days."

Gaye's early gospel-tinged records reflected these feelings. But both he and Gordy were to make many musical refinements in the years to come. In time, Gaye was to prove himself a talented songwriter and producer. But for a number of years, he flourished under the impressive stable of staff songwriters/producers that Gordy had gathered.

With Smokey Robinson, Marvin Gaye recorded "I'll be Doggone" and "Ain't That Peculiar." With Holland, Dozier, and Holland—best known for their

Marvin Gaye—
all his phases
were great.

work with the Supremes and the Four Tops—he made "Can I Get a Witness" and "How Sweet It Is." With Nicholas Ashford and Valerie Simpson, who later became recording stars in their own right, he and Tammy Terrell recorded the fine duets "Ain't No Mountain High Enough" and "You're All I Need to Get By." With Norman Whitfield, who also produced the Temptations, Marvin recorded an innovative version of "I Heard It through the Grapevine."

No matter who the producer or what the style, Marvin Gaye never lost his distinctive vocal sound. Though he was Motown's most commercially successful male singer in the sixties, he wasn't given complete artistic control over one of his own albums until the early seventies. The result was *What's Goin' On*, a landmark in popular music and Motown's first true concept album. The record established Gaye as one of the most creative talents in the Motown organization. According to Bobby Robinson, Marvin had complained that until *What's Goin' On,* he was never allowed enough freedom at Motown:

> Marvin once told me: "People want me to do certain things that are commercial, but I don't care about being commercial at all. I have to sing what I feel and hear. That is what I want to do." Marvin felt that Motown kept him in a straitjacket to a degree. The first thing he did when he got the chance was to produce *What's Goin' On.* That was a revolutionary record, especially for Motown. All his phases were great, but that was the real Marvin Gaye.

Marvin Gaye wasn't the only Motown artist who wanted more control over his product. But in Berry Gordy's hit record production-line concept, producers usually had more control than the singers themselves. This approach really began to pay off for Gordy in 1963, when one of his best producer/songwriter teams—Lamont Dozier and Brian and Eddie Holland—had a hit with Martha and the Vandellas called "Heat Wave." A follow-up record, "Dancin' in the Streets," was an even bigger hit. But this was only the beginning of an amazing three-year stretch that was to yield twenty-eight top-20 hits for the trio. Here's how *The Rolling Stone History of Rock and Roll* described Holland, Dozier, and Holland's style:

> . . . [While] the vocalists provided emotion, the band mounted a nonstop percussive assault highlighted by a "hot" mix, with shrill, hissing cymbals and a booming bass—anything to make a song jump out of a car radio.

> With tambourines rattling to a blistering 4-4 beat, the H-D-H sound . . . came to epitomize what Motown would call "The Sound of Young America" . . . Holland-Dozier-Holland did nothing less than make [this] formula a work of art itself. . . .

The success of Holland, Dozier, and Holland seemed to coincide with the development of a readily identifiable Motown sound. Berry Gordy was a man who believed in sticking with a winning formula. His pattern of releasing records had always been to follow up a hit song with one that sounded almost exactly the same. Only after a particular release started to slip in popularity would Gordy attempt to change the sound. This formula was highly successful with groups like the Temptations and the Four Tops, but it reached its commercial peak with three skinny girls from Detroit's Brewster housing projects who called themselves the Supremes.

Even before Berry Gordy let Diana Ross and her two friends cut a record, he sensed something special about her. Gordy may have started his empire with blues and soul, but he envisioned his acts working swanky nightclubs in Las Vegas and New York. Those same wealthy adults who found real rhythm and blues too tough for their tastes might readily pay to see and hear a black act—if it was packaged properly.

Diana Ross, in spite of her great success, wasn't the best female singer at Motown. There were even some who felt that one of the other Supremes, Mary Wilson, should have been the group's lead singer. But Gordy sensed that Diana could take him to the top of the entertainment business, if he only could find the right sound. After a couple of flops, Gordy and Hol-

Diana Ross and the Supremes—Berry Gordy's dream group.

land, Dozier, and Holland finally found the perfect song.

"Where Did Our Love Go" was more than just a great song, it was the ideal vehicle for Diana Ross's youthful, breathy, sexy voice. If she had some limitations as a singer, this song made them seem like strengths. As Jamaica Kinkaid wrote in the *Village Voice:*

> ... No girl anywhere ever sounded like that. It was the voice of a young girl wanting everything, yet not knowing what it was that she wanted or what it was that she would get. . . . I think you had to be a teenage girl or a teenage boy wanting teenage girls to understand what she meant. She was awfully subtle and decent, yet she seemed to promise everything.

At last, Berry Gordy had found the sound and the image he needed to complete his master plan. For openers, he would work the sound Holland, Dozier, and Holland had gotten on "Where Did Our Love Go" to the hilt. Within a year, Diana and her friends had followed their first hit with five more million-selling singles: "Baby Love," "Stop! In the Name of Love," "Come See about Me," "Back in My Arms Again," and "I Hear a Symphony." Never before had any group ever had six million-selling records in such a short period of time. Together with the other successful Motown artists, the Supremes helped make Motown the company with the highest total record sales in 1964.

Now that Gordy had found an act whose look and sound truly transcended all boundaries of race, he began to groom his charges for what he considered bigger and better things. As soon as Gordy had secured a dominant position on the record charts, he started grooming his acts for "high class" nightclubs. Records like *The Four Tops on Broadway* and *The Temptations in a Mellow Mood* reinforced this push toward so-called respectability. Gordy also required his acts to attend a kind of in-house finishing school called "International Talent Management Incorporated." I.T.M.I.'s function was to teach Motown acts how to walk, talk, and dress with the kind of grace nightclub audiences expected.

In spite of these obvious attempts at regimentation and respectability, there was still some good rhythm and blues being recorded at Motown in the second half of the sixties. One of the best and unique artists to be recorded during this period was a singing saxophone player named Junior Walker. Like the majority of Motown artists, Junior had some good years when the label was thriving, but saw the hits tail

Junior Walker—
Motown's only
instrumental star.

off in the seventies. Undaunted, he is still one of the
best and unique live rhythm and blues performers
around. Junior lights up when he talks about Motown
in its heyday.

> Motown was doing its best stuff in the sixties, and there
> was so much of it. Every time someone had a hit, that
> would make the other people work harder. It would
> make you feel a little jealous. But in the end, all the
> different people getting hits made you work harder and
> feel better. I'd say about Diana Ross, "That girl's gettin' a
> lot of hits. I gotta get in there and get me another hit to
> keep up with her." Then my group would come back

with another record and get back up there with them and then they would come back with another hit record. In those days, the atmosphere was competitive, but it was mostly a friendly kind of competition.

As Motown's only instrumental star, Junior Walker was, in his way, the label's most individualistic artist. While he is a skilled and highly appealing rhythm and blues singer, Junior's greatest strength has always been his unique style on the tenor sax. There has never been a better and more original rhythm and blues honker. Junior's style is grounded in the blues, a grounding that even the most skilled imitator can't duplicate.

"When I was growing up," Junior remembers, "I used to listen to a lot of records by country bluesmen like Sonny Boy Williamson. By the time I got into playing myself, I had heard that style so much, I could play in naturally. Someone could try to copy that sound, but then it would be just like something thrown together. People who know what they're listening to want things to really be rooted in real feelings and experiences. You'd have to come up from under there to get that feeling and that sound."

Like many important rhythm and blues artists at Motown and elsewhere, Junior got a good deal of his musical grounding in gospel music. Though he is not a particularly religious man, Junior considers the religious part of his musical background invaluable.

When I was a kid in Arkansas, I was made to go to church and listen to that music. Some of those singers really got into it in a way that gave me a lot of musical ideas. The main thing about spiritual singers is that they sing from their heart. That's why there's so much feel-

ing in that music. When I do a song, I sometimes remember how those singers in church sang them.
There's a lot of that in my sax playing because I heard it
every Sunday . . .

Junior Walker and the All-Stars had a series of
hits on Motown that were essentially half instrumental and half vocal. Junior developed this sound before
he came to Motown, and was one of the few artists
whose success seemed to be based more on his own
natural sound that on some premeditated production
formula. On songs like "Shotgun," "Roadrunner,"
and "Shoot Your Shot," Junior would start off with a
rousing sax solo and then launch into a raspy, catchy
vocal chorus. He recalls how he first developed the
formula that became his trademark:

> When I started, I didn't know what style I was in. . . .
> Once, we were playing in a club and a lot of people were
> dancing. I said, "What kind of dance is it that you are
> doing?" They said, "Shotgun." And they said, "Why
> don't you just cut a record on it?" So I did. I called up
> Mr. Gordy and told him that I had a number I wanted to
> do. I had met him before and he told me to call him any
> time I wanted to record. He said, "Come on in and cut
> it." When I told him the name of the song was "Shot-
> gun," he fell down laughing on the phone. We cut the
> record and that was my first big hit. After that, the hits
> started coming.

After a while, sales of these danceable, blues-
based records peaked. On another label, Junior's
career might have been neglected. But the producers
at Motown succeeded in taking his basic sound and
extending it to remakes of hits previously recorded by
Marvin Gaye ("How Sweet It Is") and the Supremes

("Come See About Me"). No other record company has ever been as artistically or commercially successful at recycling its own hit songs as Motown. This accomplishment is even more remarkable given the quality of both the original records and the later renditions.

Junior Walker may not be in a class with Marvin Gaye as a distinctive rhythm and blues singer, yet Junior's remake of "How Sweet It Is" is as memorable as Marvin's original. Instead of trying to duplicate the controlled studio sound of the original record, Junior's producer, Johnny Bristol, managed to achieve the effect of opening a door and walking into a party that was in full swing. Junior recalls how that feeling was achieved:

> At first, Johnny Bristol wanted me to sing "How Sweet It Is" like Marvin Gaye, but I said, "Hey man, you know that I can't sing like Marvin, but I can do it my own way." After a little arguing, Johnny said, "Go ahead and do it the way you want. . . ." That party feeling was the idea of the people who were coordinating the session. The producers at Motown always had a lot of good ideas. They used that party sound on a lot of my records. When I heard it, I was happy with that sound. I said, "Wow, they really made that thing sound better by adding the voices of people partying to it."

A few years later, the producers at Motown took Junior in another direction, one that was to prove his most commercially successful. Instead of danceable blues, they employed a medium-tempo ballad feel. Nevertheless, the now-patented All-Star formula of play a chorus, sing a chorus was used in pretty much the same way as it had been on "Shotgun" and "Road

Runner." Junior remembers that both he and Berry Gordy had their doubts about the commercial potential of Junior Walker recording ballads. But the success of "What Does It Take" took Junior and the All-Stars into a whole new phase.

> Johnny Bristol wanted me to do "What Does It Take." I didn't want to do it, and was stalling him off for a whole year. Finally, he insisted. He said, "Look, I want you to do this tune." There was a big discussion about whether or not I should record it. Mr. Gordy didn't really feel that it was what I should be doing at the time and I felt the same way. But Johnny thought it was a big change for the better. So we decided to put it in the album. And it broke out. It surprised me and Mr. Gordy and a lot of people at Motown. After that, they decided that I should record more slow tunes.

By the early seventies, Motown was no longer dominating the charts. Berry Gordy seemed preoccupied with producing films and personally guiding Diana Ross's career. Around this time, many of Motown's best artists began to leave the label for more lucrative arrangements elsewhere. There was one artist, though, whom Berry Gordy knew he could not afford to lose.

Stevie Wonder, blind and only twelve years old, had signed with the label in the early sixties. Nine years after his first hit, "Fingertips," became a number-one record, Stevie still had little control over his music. He also was getting what he considered less than a fair shake financially.

Like many Motown recording artists, Stevie had signed on when he was very young and hungry to make his mark as a performer. The contract he signed set up a kind of parent-child relationship in which the company had total control over all musical and financial decisions. It was reported, for example, that even after he had reached the top of the charts with "Fingertips," Stevie was only receiving an allowance of $2.50 a week.

All told, Stevie had earned approximately one million dollars during his first ten years at Motown, most of which was put in trust. This is a large sum of money by everyday standards. But when you have sold thirty million dollars' worth of records, as Stevie did during that period, the million-dollar figure seems less than overwhelming. As Bobby Robinson explains:

> A lot of Motown artists became upset with their financial arrangements after a few years. Some left the label because of that. Motown had a strict salary thing, which people accepted at the beginning because they were young and wanted to break in. A new artist will take anything just to get started. But when you get into the good life and see what's going on you're just not willing to accept that. . . .

Even among all the great Motown artists, Stevie Wonder stood out as an exceptional talent, one who is often described as a genius. Like most of the Motown acts, his early records were a deft mixture of blues and gospel roots. But Stevie soon displayed an unusual versatility. He was one of the first black artists to record songs by major rock songwriters—like the Beatles' "We Can Work It Out" and Bob Dylan's "Blowin' in the Wind."

Stevie also wrote much of his own material, here again demonstrating skills in a variety of musical

Stevie Wonder—
one artist
Motown could
not afford to
lose.

bags. "My Cherie Amour" showed the softer side of
Stevie, while "Signed, Sealed and Delivered" was a
masterpiece of danceable soul music. But Stevie was
growing increasingly upset because, though he was
writing many of his own songs, others were receiving
the credit.

By the time Stevie turned twenty-one, he was not
content to be just another obedient member of the
"Motown Family." He was ready to make his move.
"I'm twenty-one now," he told one Motown executive.
"I'm not going to do what you want anymore. Void
my contract." Stevie then took several hundred
thousand dollars of his own money and produced his
own album at New York's Electric Lady Studios.

The result of Stevie's efforts was an album called *Music of My Mind*. This album was revolutionary in a number of ways. Stevie did about ninety-five percent of all the playing and singing himself. He had mastered the synthesizer, a keyboard which is capable of reproducing the sounds of other instruments, and used it as the main instrument on the album. The songs on *Music of My Mind* were unlike any Stevie had done before. It was a true concept album, reminiscent in some ways of the Beatles' *Revolver.* Stevie used elements of jazz and rock 'n' roll, as well as rhythm and blues, to create this truly original work. When he was through, he went back to Motown to talk business.

Berry Gordy had always been a tough businessman, but he was no fool. He was smart enough to recognize that Stevie Wonder had the potential to be Motown's most important artist for the next twenty years. Although he must have cringed at the thought of shelling out the kind of bucks Stevie was demanding, Gordy really had no choice at the time. Stevie was simply too good and too prolific to let go.

As the years went by, Gordy seemed less willing to match the kind of deal he had given Stevie Wonder with other artists. Michael Jackson, another twelve-year-old genius who, with his brothers, had signed with the label in the early seventies, was allowed to leave. He was joined by Marvin Gaye and Diana Ross during the next few years. Junior Walker also left the label around the same time as the others. And though his talents have not diminished over the years, Junior's records haven't graced the charts for over a decade. Junior talked about his leaving Motown and his frustrations in the years that followed.

I left Motown around 1978. They were turning out product all through the seventies, but they were not promoting it. For a while, Diana was doing real good and Berry Gordy was much more into her and her movies than into pushing his other recording artists. Many of those artists just seemed to get lost at Motown, and I guess I was one of them. After a while, I felt it was time to move on and try something else. I signed with [producer] Norman Whitfield and Warner Records. We did this album called *Backstreet Boogie* there. One of the songs from the album, "Wishing On A Star," even got a Grammy nomination, but Warner's didn't push it enough. I'm recording right now and waiting to see what is going to happen with Warner Brothers. If that doesn't work out, I'll probably just get with another record company and more or less just produce myself.

Motown taught me a lot about the record business, about recording and releasing records. I am thankful that I did go that way and for what I have learned. . . . I learned a lot from the way Mr. Gordy did things . . . not only in business, but also in the recording studio. Of all the studios I've worked in, I've still never gotten that kind of special feeling I did during those great years at Motown.

Though Motown is no longer what it once was, it is still an important label, with artists like Rick James, Lionel Richie, the Commodores, as well as Smokey Robinson and Stevie Wonder. While it may never again wield the tremendous power that it did during its "golden decade" (1962–71), the music that Berry Gordy and his talented producers, songwriters, and singers created has left an indelible mark not only on rhythm and blues, but on popular music in general. As writers Joe McEwen and Jim Miller put it in *The Rolling Stone Illustrated History of Rock and Roll:*

Nicholas Ashford and Valerie Simpson—Motown
songwriting/producing team who became hit
artists on other labels.

... The Motown hits of the sixties revolutionized American popular music. ... Never again would black popular
music be dismissed as a minority taste. For more than a
decade, Berry Gordy and his many talented cohorts
managed . . . to translate . . . [black music] into "The
Sound of Young America." [Artistically] as well as commercially, Motown's achievement will likely remain un-
rivaled for years to come.

## MOTOWN SELECTED DISCOGRAPHY

(Note—All releases on Motown subsidiaries such as Tamla and Gordy are listed as Motown)

### THE COMMODORES

Greatest Hits. . . . . . . . . . . . . . . . . . . . . . . . . . . . . . . . . . . Motown
In the Pocket. . . . . . . . . . . . . . . . . . . . . . . . . . . . . . . . . . Motown
Machine Gun . . . . . . . . . . . . . . . . . . . . . . . . . . . . . . . . . . Motown
Midnight Maybe. . . . . . . . . . . . . . . . . . . . . . . . . . . . . . . Motown
Lionel Richie . . . . . . . . . . . . . . . . . . . . . . . . . . . . . . . . . . Motown

### THE FOUR TOPS

Anthology. . . . . . . . . . . . . . . . . . . . . . . . . . . . . . . . . . . . . Motown
The Best of the Four Tops . . . . . . . . . . . . . . . . . . . . . . . . Motown
The Four Tops . . . . . . . . . . . . . . . . . . . . . . . . . . . . . . . . . Motown
Greatest Hits—Volumes I and II . . . . . . . . . . . . . . . . . . Motown
Motown Special . . . . . . . . . . . . . . . . . . . . . . . . . . . . . . . Motown

### MARVIN GAYE

Anthology. . . . . . . . . . . . . . . . . . . . . . . . . . . . . . . . . . . . . Motown
Greatest Hits. . . . . . . . . . . . . . . . . . . . . . . . . . . . . . . . . . Motown
Soulful Mood . . . . . . . . . . . . . . . . . . . . . . . . . . . . . . . . . Motown
Superhits. . . . . . . . . . . . . . . . . . . . . . . . . . . . . . . . . . .,. . Motown
United with Tammy Terrell . . . . . . . . . . . . . . . . . . . . . . . Motown
What's Going On. . . . . . . . . . . . . . . . . . . . . . . . . . . . . . . Motown

### THE JACKSONS

ABC with the Jackson 5 . . . . . . . . . . . . . . . . . . . . . . . . . . Motown
Anthology. . . . . . . . . . . . . . . . . . . . . . . . . . . . . . . . . . . . . Motown
The Best of Michael Jackson . . . . . . . . . . . . . . . . . . . . . . Motown
Golden Greats . . . . . . . . . . . . . . . . . . . . . . . . . . . . . . . . . Motown
Greatest Hits. . . . . . . . . . . . . . . . . . . . . . . . . . . . . . . . . . Motown
I Want You Back. . . . . . . . . . . . . . . . . . . . . . . . . . . . . . . . Motown
Jackson 5 Greatest Hits . . . . . . . . . . . . . . . . . . . . . . . . . . Motown
Motown Special . . . . . . . . . . . . . . . . . . . . . . . . . . . . . . . Motown
Diana Ross Presents the Jackson 5 . . . . . . . . . . . . . . . . . Motown

## RICK JAMES
Come Get It ..................................... Motown
Rick James .................................... Motown
Reflections .................................... Motown
Stone City Band ............................... Motown

## GLADYS KNIGHT AND THE PIPS
Anthology...................................... Motown

## MARTHA AND THE VANDELLAS
Anthology...................................... Motown
Come and Get Your Memories .................... Motown
Dance Party ................................... Motown
Greatest Hits.................................. Motown

## SMOKEY ROBINSON AND THE MIRACLES
Anthology...................................... Motown
Greatest Hits—Volumes I and II .................. Motown
Hi We're the Miracles .......................... Motown
Miracles from the Beginning .................... Motown

## DIANA ROSS AND THE SUPREMES
Diana All The Greatest Hits ..................... Motown
Hits by the Supremes........................... Motown
Meet the Supremes ............................. Motown
Diana Ross Anthology .......................... Motown
Diana Ross and the Supremes Anthology ........... Motown
Diana Ross's Greatest Hits ..................... Motown
Diana Ross and the Supremes' Greatest Hits ....... Motown
Diana Ross and the Supremes Join the Temptations ..... Motown
The Supremes Sing Holland Dozier Holland ......... Motown
Touch Me in the Morning (Solo)................... Motown

## THE TEMPTATIONS
Anthology—1964–1973.......................... Motown
Greatest Hits—Volumes I, II, and III .............. Motown
Meet the Temptations........................... Motown
The Temptations Sing Smokey Robinson ........... Motown

## JUNIOR WALKER

Anthology . . . . . . . . . . . . . . . . . . . . . . . . . . . . . . . . . . . . . . . . Motown
Greatest Hits—Volumes I and II . . . . . . . . . . . . . . . . . . . Motown
Motown Special . . . . . . . . . . . . . . . . . . . . . . . . . . . . . . . . . . Motown

## MARY WELLS

Bye Bye Baby . . . . . . . . . . . . . . . . . . . . . . . . . . . . . . . . . . . Motown
Greatest Hits . . . . . . . . . . . . . . . . . . . . . . . . . . . . . . . . . . . . Motown
Vintage Stock . . . . . . . . . . . . . . . . . . . . . . . . . . . . . . . . . . . Motown

## STEVIE WONDER

Anthology . . . . . . . . . . . . . . . . . . . . . . . . . . . . . . . . . . . . . . . Motown
For Once in My Life . . . . . . . . . . . . . . . . . . . . . . . . . . . . . . Motown
Greatest Hits . . . . . . . . . . . . . . . . . . . . . . . . . . . . . . . . . . . . Motown
Innervisions . . . . . . . . . . . . . . . . . . . . . . . . . . . . . . . . . . . . . Motown
Music of My Mind . . . . . . . . . . . . . . . . . . . . . . . . . . . . . . . Motown
Signed, Sealed and Delivered . . . . . . . . . . . . . . . . . . . . . . Motown
Songs in the Key of Life . . . . . . . . . . . . . . . . . . . . . . . . . . Motown
Talking Book . . . . . . . . . . . . . . . . . . . . . . . . . . . . . . . . . . . Motown
12-Year-Old Genius . . . . . . . . . . . . . . . . . . . . . . . . . . . . . . Motown

# CHAPTER 8

# SOUL MUSIC

## The Sound of the Sixties

*Say it loud—I'm black and I'm proud*

—James Brown

It's 1967, and I've got a ticket to what promises to be one of the best concerts of the year—Otis Redding and the Buffalo Springfield at the Fillmore East. It's not just that the Otis is my favorite soul singer and that the Springfield is one of the best rock groups around. It's the combination that blows my mind. Otis Redding—a transformed gospel singer if there ever was one—somehow captivating the young white audience on his own terms. And the Buffalo Springfield—Neil Young, Stephen Stills, and a bunch of other white hippies, who some people thought of as America's answer to the Beatles. That kind of bill could have happened only during an era like the sixties. But in fact, it never did happen. Someone canceled out of the concert, and a few months later, Otis Redding died in a plane crash.

Otis Redding's death was just one of the tragedies that prevented the total merging of black and white musical styles that was in the wind during the sixties. Worse yet, the decline of soul music came to symbolize the collapse of an overriding spirit of hope and social change that affected black and white people at that time. There were so many things in the air in the sixties. The awakening of black pride, the growing civil rights activism among whites, the anti-Vietnam movement, and, of course, the music—that sweet soul music.

The debate over the meaning of *soul*—like that over the term *rhythm and blues* itself—has heated up over the years. There are some who saw it as the

Otis Redding—embodies the spirit of soul.

emergence of a new black consciousness, a sense of pride and togetherness that seemed to coalesce in the sixties. In black urban communities like New York's Harlem and Chicago's South Side, it wasn't just a new musical sound that people called soul, but a whole new way of thinking about being black. Here's how writer Al Calloway described the style of soul in *Esquire* magazine:

> . . . The sixties have ushered in a "new" mood with a significant number of soul brothers and sisters, causing a clean break with "anything other than who you really are. . . ." The style of soul is getting back into the African folk bag. . . . In Harlem, soul brothers wear pieces of

ivory in their ears and ornament their noses like the
Yorubas of West Africa. . . . Soul is what, forever, has
made black people hip. And it is what has enticed whites
to imitate them without understanding it. Among black
people, soul is a congenital understanding and respect
for each other. It is the knowledge that one is a *segment*
of all that is. . . . It makes you humble, peaceful. That is
why, above all, soul is wise and weary. It is the self-
perception that informs you how and when to groove in
your own way while others groove in theirs, and it is the
sophistication that knows better than to ask, "Understand me," and settles instead for, "Don't mess with me."

While the golden period of soul music coincided
with the growth of black pride and black militancy,
the music itself was good-natured and sweet. The
three record labels that specialized in soul all used the
black church as their starting points. Bobby Robinson, who produced one of the first instrumental soul
hits—King Curtis's "Soul Twist"—describes the foundation of soul this way:

Soul came from gospel music and blues—the real music
of black people. It came out of the suffering and desola-
tion and the kind of life that they lived, and the conditions they lived under. The prejudice of having to go
through the back door . . . things in the recesses of my
mind that I saw when I was growing up. That was really
an exclusive black experience, and the music that came
out of it was an authentic folk form.

Many of the great soul artists of the sixties were
recorded by Atlantic Records or by the Memphis-
based Stax/Volt label that eventually became an Atlantic affiliate. Like the Motown sound, soul at Atlantic and Stax had its roots in the black church. And

while the freedom to express one's feelings with a gospel fervor may have been liberating to the growing crop of soul singers, the words to most of the memorable songs of that era spoke not of social protest, but about romantic or physical love.

Most of the great soul singers had their own special way of handling this topic. At Atlantic, Wilson Pickett became known for a raspy, sexual approach in hard-driving songs like "Midnight Hour" and "Mustang Sally." Percy Sledge, on the other hand, took a more romantic, philosophical approach in songs like "When A Man Loves A Woman" and "Take Time to Know Her." At Stax, Sam and Dave often bragged of their prowess as lovers in songs like "Hold On, I'm Coming" and "Soul Man." Otis Redding became known as "Mr. Pitiful" because of the many times he was hurt in his songs. And though he wrote "Respect," a song that Aretha Franklin would later turn in to something much more militant, Otis was simply talking about what he wanted from his woman when he got home.

While all these soul singers were strongly rooted in the black experience, they were speaking about matters that went beyond questions of race. After all, love songs had long been the mainstay of all popular music, yet soul music was different from anything that came before it. So great was the sound of soul music that you didn't have to be black, or even sympathetic to blacks, in order to dig it.

In England, musicians like Lennon and McCartney and Jagger and Richards became serious students of rhythm and blues. Still, they weren't necessarily concerned about, or even aware of, the relation be-

**Sam and Dave—togetherness.**

tween the oppression of blacks in America and the great music they created. For no apparent sociological reason, these English musicians just liked what they heard and used it to formulate their own sound.

As some of the more successful British groups began touring America, they started to get a first-hand taste of the racial tension in this country. Eric Burdon, former lead singer of the British rhythm and blues group the Animals, once told an interviewer that he was baffled when he met a Southern white girl who loved Otis Redding's music although she disliked blacks in general.

Racial hypocrisy aside, the shared culture of soul music came to include white as well as black listeners. To a great extent, however, it was through white English rock bands that young American listeners came to appreciate the style. The recycling of soul songs by groups like the Beatles and Rolling Stones brought people like James Brown, Otis Redding, and Wilson Pickett to the attention of many white kids.

Many of the early Beatles records were covers of rhythm and blues classics, with an emphasis on gospel-tinged soul music. These included "Twist and Shout" (The Isley Brothers), "Please Mr. Postman" (The Marvelettes), and "You've Really Got a Hold on Me" (Smokey Robinson and the Miracles). Even though the Beatles' versions of these songs were done mostly with guitars in a rock-band format, they were very close to the originals. Still, there was enough of a difference in their sound to attract many new listeners.

The Rolling Stones intentionally cultivated an image that was quite the opposite of the Beatles'. Rather than going for a clean-cut, witty image, the Stones came across as a streetwise, sexy rock group that your mother wouldn't like. Their early songs came directly from bluesmen like Muddy Waters and Elmore James. And over the years, they have recorded songs by soulmen like the Temptations, Smokey and the Miracles, Marvin Gaye, and Solomon Burke. Mick Jagger was never a great singer and his band was sometimes sloppy and out of tune. Yet his musical feel and attitude made him tremendously popular with white listeners—even those who bought the original blues and soul artists.

The Beatles, the Rolling Stones.

When Otis Redding recorded his own version of the Stones' "Satisfaction," he became the first established soul artist to have a hit song written by rock songwriters. Not that this was necessary to prove the interplay between blacks and whites in the creation of soul music; although most of the great soul singers were black, many of the musicians and record producers were white. In fact, the most important soul songwriter and record producer outside of Motown was a white guitarist named Steve Cropper.

At the heart of what came to be called *the Memphis Sound* was a four-piece racially mixed band called Bookter T. and the MG's. Steve Cropper—the band's guitarist—co-wrote Otis Redding's "Dock of the Bay," and Wilson Pickett's "Midnight Hour." He was the producer on virtually all of Otis Redding's records as well as the man responsible for the hot guitar licks on such soul classics as Sam and Dave's "Soul Man." But in spite of his own considerable contributions and those of his other collaborators, Cropper made no bones about whom he believed to be the most important man in soul music. As he told an interviewer in 1967:

> Otis is the only one I can think of now who does it best. He gets over to the people what he is talking about, and he does it in so few words that if you read them on paper they might not make any sense. But when you hear the way he sings them, you know exactly what he is talking about.

Bobby Robinson agrees with Steve Cropper's statement, but he feels that there is more that needs to be said in talking about Otis Redding's contribution to soul music in general, and to the Memphis sound in particular.

When you talk about the Memphis sound, you're talking about Otis. He invented it. Memphis didn't really have a readily identifiable sound before Otis . . . Booker T. and the MG's were important, but Otis usually told them what to play. . . . He was one of the few artists who had the potential to really bring black and white audiences together.

Otis Redding was a very special talent. He was a gifted singer-songwriter, a dynamic live performer, and a skilled craftsman in the recording studio. Yet, as he told *Hit Parader*'s Jim Delehant, he was discovered more or less by accident.

I used to be a well driller. I made a dollar twenty-five an hour, drilling wells in Macon, Georgia. One day I drove a friend of mine, Johnny Jenkins, up to a recording session [at Stax Records in Memphis]. They had thirty minutes left in the studio and I asked if I could do a song, "These Arms of Mine." They did it and it sold about eight hundred thousand copies. I've been going strong ever since.

"These Arms of Mine" was the kind of slow, soulful ballad that first brought Otis to the attention of black audiences. Though his voice was full and throaty, his phrasings reminded listeners of the smooth-voiced Sam Cooke. Otis's career really took off when he recorded "Satisfaction" and a series of up-tempo originals that included "Respect" and "Security." After a triumphant appearance at the Monterey festival and an ecstatically received European tour, Otis seemed ready to move on to even greater heights.

For several months, there had been talk that Otis had taken the Stax sound to another place. A single—

"(Sittin' on the) Dock of the Bay"—was going to be the song that would usher in a new phase in the accept-ance of soul music. And though the song was to be-come Otis's first number-one record, the man himself died in a plane crash only a few days before "Dock of the Bay" was released. He was only twenty-seven years old. Shortly after his death, *Rolling Stone* ran the following eulogy:

> In 1967 [Otis Redding] proved himself to be a master of production . . . and a writer whose material was not only suited to himself but to the entire medium. His voice was rough, but it carried with it a style and a grace and an originality that was rare in the field of rhythm and blues, rock and roll, rock and soul or whatever it's called. Otis was a man of music.
>
> The Memphis sound was going to take over soul in 1968. Everyone knew it, and Otis was the [main] man at Stax. In 1968, he was going to become "The King of them all, y'all."
>
> Otis was the Crown Prince of Soul, and now the Crown Prince is dead.

As great as Otis Redding was, his position as the dominant force in soul music was being challenged— even before his death—by a woman. Ironically, the song that was to make Aretha Franklin the undis-puted Queen of Soul was an Otis Redding song called "Respect."

Though Aretha was younger than Otis Redding, she had been making records for years before Otis showed up at the Stax Recording studios. Aretha's father, the Reverend C. L. Franklin, was one of the most successful and influential gospel ministers in America. The head of Detroit's New Bethel Baptist

Church, the Reverend Mr. Franklin was the major figure in that city's gospel community. Aretha's mother was also a respected gospel performer.

Whenever top gospel artists like Mahalia Jackson, Clara Ward, and James Cleveland were in Detroit, they stayed at the Franklin home. Spurred on by the encouragement of these famous performers, Aretha began recording gospel music for the Chess label at the age of fourteen. A few years later, Sam Cooke—another former gospel star who had made his fortune in popular music—advised Aretha to pursue a similar path.

After signing with Columbia Records in 1961, Aretha spent the next five years working with different producers in a variety of popular styles. Although she made some good records during that period, her producers at Columbia couldn't seem to find a style that would maximize her talents or her commercial potential. When her contract was up, Aretha signed on with Atlantic Records, a label that specialized in soul.

Jerry Wexler, Aretha's producer at Atlantic, never had any doubt about the right musical direction for his new artist. "I put her back in church" is the way he has often described what he did for Aretha. Instead of trying to mold her into a pop singer or a jazz singer, Wexler went with the one type of music the producers at Columbia had neglected—gospel-based, hard-hitting soul.

Wexler took Aretha to Fame Studios in Muscle Shoals, Alabama, a place that was both geographically and musically close to Stax. Wexler centered the music around Aretha's voice and piano. Aretha's sisters Erma and Carolyn provided rousing background vocals, while the Muscle Shoals house band offered perfect support. The music that came out of those sessions was more than just Aretha Franklin at her best and most natural. It was some of the finest soul ever recorded. In a conversation with *Record World* magazine, Jerry Wexler talked about the artist whose voice he calls "the best I ever heard in my life":

> I never imagined I'd have the good luck to sign [Aretha]. It was too good to be true. . . . I also didn't realize what a good piano player she was. And I started her playing a lot more piano on my records. . . .
>
> She had a lot of songs for her first album. "I Never Loved a Man" (her first single and the title of her first album) was written by Ronnie Shannon, a Detroit songwriter. She came in with that. She had the whole arrangement, and the whole idea of it, and it was just thrilling to hear. . . .
>
> I thought "I Never Loved A Man" was an R&B hit. I was willing to settle for that for the first record, that would have been fine. . . . [The record eventually became a top-ten pop hit.]
>
> "Respect" was her next single. That was a Grammy winner. It was a pop [hit]. I can't take any credit for that. She did it, she surprised me. She just went and did it. . . . We would come in to the studio, and she would have six or eight songs all ready to go, and this was one. She'd have the layout, the piano part and the vocal backgrounds. So we just had to fill in the instruments—very little change.
>
> I played a test of her version of "Respect" for Otis Redding. He said, "I just lost my song. That girl took it away from me." He said it in a spirit of generosity. He was thrilled with the record. . . . Also, it's sort of the keynote record of the time. There were intimations of Women's Lib at the time. . . .

Aretha Franklin—so good she overwhelmed an entire musical style.

Aretha kept on turning out great soul hits for a few more years, sometimes experimenting with renditions of songs like the Beatles' "Let It Be" and the Band's "The Weight." After a time, though, it seemed as if Aretha was trying to redefine her musical direction. Soon, syrupy strings replaced gospel pianos, and Aretha appeared to have lost her musical center. Almost two decades after she recorded "Respect," Aretha still may be the best soul singer around. But for whatever reason, she hasn't made a single record that approaches the quality of those early Atlantic cuts.

Perhaps, as some critics have suggested, Aretha's early Atlantic Records were so great that they created a standard that neither she, nor any other soul singer, could live up to. As Peter Guralnick observes in *The Rolling Stone Illustrated History of Rock and Roll:*

> [Aretha's first sessions in Muscle Shoals] in a way was the end of soul proper. Not that it vanished in a puff of smoke. . . . Nor was Aretha's style any radical departure from the soul sound that had preceded it. . . . No, it wasn't so much that Aretha departed from a style as by her genius she defined it. Her success, both artistic and commercial, swept everything in its wake. . . . [Though there has been a sprinkling of soul over the years] the sense of common purpose which had animated the movement for three or four years was gone. . . .

It may seem a little farfetched to conceive of an artist so powerful that she could blow away an entire musical style. And in fact, there were more important factors that helped bring the golden era of soul to a premature end. Otis Redding's death and Aretha Franklin's musical triumph coincided with a distinct change in America's social climate.

The most important single event may have been the assassination of Martin Luther King, Jr., in April 1968. Malcolm X had met a similar fate a few years earlier. And Bobby Kennedy—a champion of civil rights—was the victim of an assassin's bullet just a few months after the King tragedy. But the Reverend Martin Luther King's demise was especially significant because he was the first black leader to bring the fervor of gospel music into the political arena. King's oratory style was highlighted by the same kind of phrasing and musical dynamics that great rhythm and blues singers used; and his message of hope set the tone for the soul era.

All of this senseless killing created a more paranoid, violent atmosphere in America—one that wasn't reflected in the sweet sounds of soul. As Peter Guralnick notes: "The soul movement was [based] too much upon an assumption of good faith to survive the shock of that awakening." Thus, after 1968, the music became far more aggressive and socially self-conscious than it had been during its formative years.

Black artists who wanted to incorporate elements of violence and social consciousness into their music didn't have to go far to find those influences. Many white rock bands were dominated by loud, screeching electric guitars, while others were focused in on social protest. There were two men who were ingenious enough to combine these elements with soul music in the late sixties—Jimi Hendrix and Sylvester Stewart (aka Sly Stone).

The short but brilliant career of Jimi Hendrix was filled with irony. Though he was probably the most accomplished blues musician of his generation, his influence is felt more in heavy metal than in any other musical style. Jimi was a black man thoroughly rooted in black musical styles, yet he was never able to find real acceptance among black audiences. This was a rather strange turnaround in an era when black performers were doing everything in their power to appeal to white listeners.

During the earlier stages of his career, Hendrix had made a name for himself as a backup musician on the soul circuit, but he had greater ambitions. After years of playing behind such great rhythm and blues vocalists as Little Richard and Otis Redding, Hendrix was convinced that he could not compete as a singer. But after seeing how far Bob Dylan and others had gotten with limited vocal equipment, he decided to give it a shot.

Jimi Hendrix couldn't—as they say in the music business—get arrested. He was turned down by virtually every American record company. Then, he hooked up with Chas Chandler, an English manager who once played bass with the Animals. Chandler believed that Jimi would be a sensation in England, a country that was obsessed with blues guitar playing. Hendrix formed a band called the Experience with two English musicians, drummer Mitch Mitchell and bass guitarist Noel Redding. All three musicians grew electric hair, wore freaky clothes, and played some of the loudest, most aggressive music anyone had ever heard.

Hendrix and his band were an immediate hit in England with three chart-topping singles: "Hey Joe," "The Wind Cries Mary," and "Fifty-first Anniversary." Soon, he would also be the most talked-about rock musician in America. In an attempt to cover all bases, Hendrix used every trick in the book in his stage act. He played guitar behind his back, caressed the strings with his tongue, and smashed the instrument to smithereens at the end of each performance. But this was all showmanship designed to create a response and controversy. The real excitement was in the man's guitar playing. If Aretha blew all the other soul singers away with her great singing, Jimi Hendrix made a whole generation of blues guitar players feel like throwing their instruments into the garbage.

There was a whole slew of great blues guitarists on both sides of the Atlantic. Eric Clapton, Jeff Beck, and Pete Townshend were the dominant figures in England. In America, the late Mike Bloomfield was considered the top electric blues guitarist of his era. Schooled in the authentic Chicago scene, Bloomfield forged a reputation, first as the lead guitarist in the Paul Butterfield Blues Band, and then in his own group, the Electric Flag. But when he heard Hendrix, he immediately knew that he was outclassed. As Bloomfield told an interviewer from *Guitar Player* magazine:

> I was performing with Paul Butterfield, and I was the hotshot guitarist on the block—I thought I was it. . . . I went right across the street and saw him. Hendrix knew who I was, and that day, in front of my eyes, he burned me to death. I didn't even get my guitar out. H-bombs were going off, guided missiles were flying—I can't tell you the sounds he was getting out of his instrument. He was getting every sound I was ever to hear him get in that room with a Stratocaster [guitar], a Twin [small amp], a Maestro fuzz tone, and that was all—he was doing it mainly through extreme volume. How he did this, I wish I understood. He just got right up in my face with that axe [instrument], and I didn't even want to pick up a guitar for the next year.

Unfortunately, Jimi wasn't at all satisfied with his own musicianship. He was bitterly disappointed that black audiences thought of him as some kind of "jive hippy." Even though his music was clearly rooted in authentic rhythm and blues, Jimi's outlook on life and outrageous performance style were outside of what many blacks thought of as the soul tradition. Yet in many ways, Hendrix was a direct reflection of what black people in America were going through in the late sixties. As Eric Burdon told writer Tony Palmer:

> If you want to see what an American black is going through today, where his mind is at, go see Jimi Hendrix, and you'll realize why there are race riots in America and why the country is close to civil war. He's a wizard on the guitar, but his music is so disturbed and explosive. He is exorcising generations of anger.

There has been much written about the life and times of Jimi Hendrix. He lived and died in true classically destructive rock-star fashion. Yet he was much different from Janis Joplin, Jim Morrison, and Brian Jones—musicians of the same era who died young under questionable circumstances. It's not just that he was a musician far superior to any of the others. Jimi was real. His songs were real. And behind the wild stage gimmicks and crazy outfits, there was a strong message that was unmistakably real.

There were just too many things to fight in this world, too much violence, too many ugly scenes, too many ripoff artists. Jimi Hendrix represented the extreme—both in life-style and in the direction he took his music. In one of his best songs, a searing blues called "Voodoo Child," Hendrix sang these lines: "If I don't meet you no more in this world, I'll meet you in the next—don't be late." And he told an interviewer shortly before his death:

> When I die I want people to just play my music, go wild, freak out, do anything they want to do. Enjoy themselves. The mechanical life—where cities and motel rooms all merge into one—has killed that enjoyment for me. So I've got to get out. Maybe to Venus or somewhere. Some place you won't be able to find me.

Jimi Hendrix—misunderstood genius.

Jimi Hendrix left his mark on rhythm and blues and jazz. Unfortunately, though, his super-macho, electronic wizardry attracted lots of loud, unmusical imitators. Jimi was so good that he could make anything sound musical, no matter how much feedback or fuzztone he used. But most of his imitators simply did not have the talent to achieve anything close to that level of musicianship.

One other young black musician succeeded in combining elements of soul and rock into an original and commercial musical statement during the late sixties. Unlike Jimi Hendrix, whose talent seemed like some kind of cosmic gift, Sylvester (Sly Stone) Stewart's inspiration was grounded more in personal and professional experiences. A former gang leader, disk jockey, and rock producer, Sly and his band, the Family Stone, created a sound that captured the spirit of the times.

Sly seemed to understand all the musical and social undercurrents of the day. Having grown up and worked in the San Francisco area, Sly helped shape the rock style that city became famous for. He had produced several hits by the Beau Brummels as well as a record for the Great Society, a group that would later re-form as the Jefferson Airplane. But like many other producers who worked for small, independent record labels, Sly never collected any money for his hits.

Thus, in early 1967, the man who was to become the dominant figure in both rhythm and blues and rock was still unknown outside of San Francisco, though not for long. Sly was determined to organize a band that took the virtues of soul and rock a step further. With his brother on lead guitar and his sister on piano, Sly put together a sexually and racially mixed *family*. While Sly himself was the undisputed leader of the Family Stone, there was a strong sense of community in the way the band performed, as well as what their songs talked about.

The music Sly and the Family Stone made was clearly rooted in rhythm and blues and soul. At the same time, though, it had the hard edge of electric rock. This mixture of influences came naturally to the Family Stone's leader. As writer Ben Fong Torres points out in *The Rolling Stone Rock 'n' Roll Reader:*

> You must remember that Sly Stone, writing songs about blacks and whites, isn't just using rhetoric he learned in the schools. The only thing he learned in school—

outside of music theory . . . was that you learn your stuff in the streets. Sly and his family went to church together, sang in the choir together, lived in Vallejo, which Sly calls "Like a Watts, only with more whites," for twenty years together. But Sly was also a street cat, a fighting man wrestling his way through his teens.

A Sly and the Family Stone concert was *the live musical experience* of the late sixties. When they sang "Dance to the Music," you got up and danced. When they sang "Don't Call Me Nigger, Whitey, (Don't Call Me Whitey, Nigger)," you understood the pain involved in those cutting words and the relief in being able to just come on out and say what you really felt. These were just some of the ways Sly and his band brought different musical styles and cultures together. As Greil Marcus observes in his book *Mystery Train:*

> . . . What came across was not simply a new musical style, though there was that, but a shared attitude, a point of view: not just a brand-new talk, of young men and women on the move. . . .
>
> Sly's real triumph was that he had it both ways. Every nuance of his style, from the razzle-dazzle of his threads to the originality of his music to the explosiveness of his live performance, made it clear he was his own man. In the essence of his music was freedom, no one was more aggressively, creatively free than he. Yet there was room for everyone in the America of a band made up of blacks and whites, men and women, who sang out "different strokes for different folks" and were there on stage to show an audience just what such an idea of independence meant. . . .

By the end of the sixties, Sly was the major figure on the popular music scene. Suddenly, Motown was releasing records by the Temptations and a new group called the Jackson Five that were modeled on the Family Stone formula. Even jazz artists like Miles Davis seemed to be borrowing ideas from Sly. The Family Stone wasn't just a rhythm and blues phenomenon. They had, as Greil Marcus notes, broken "the color line at Woodstock, emerging as the festival's biggest hit."

In early 1970, Sly and the band cut a new single, called "Everybody Is a Star," a song of stunning originality that preached the kind of equality and love the group's music had always stood for. "Star" was, perhaps, the Family Stone's best record, and one that gave listeners hope for more of the same kind of moving, upbeat music in the future. Sly fueled these expectations when he told an interviewer that the band's next album would be their most optimistic yet.

But during the next few years, Sly's optimism would diminish, along with his popularity. Whether because of personal problems or social conditions, Sly's music took a 180-degree turn in 1971 with *There's a Riot Going On*. A grim exploration into drugs, violence, and the dark side of the black experience, *Riot* may have been the album that closed the book on sixties optimism. In any case, the best rhythm and blues records of the next few years reflected Sly's considerable musical influence. But they also mirrored his change in attitude—a change from which neither Sly nor his listeners have ever fully recovered.

## SOUL SELECTED DISCOGRAPHY

### THE ANIMALS

Greatest Hits...................................MGM
In the Beginning................................Decca

## THE BAND
Anthology......................................Capitol
The Band.......................................Capitol
Best of the Band...............................Capitol
The Last Waltz..........................Warner Brothers
Music from Big Pink............................Capitol

## THE BEATLES
The Beatles 62–66...............................Apple
The Beatles 67–70...............................Apple
The Beatles' Second Album.....................Capitol
Beatles '65....................................Capitol
The Early Beatles..............................Capitol
Introducing the Beatles........................Vee Jay
Meet the Beatles...............................Capitol
Rock 'n' Roll Music.............................Apple

## BOOKER T. AND THE MG'S
The Best of Booker T............................Stax
Pop History...................................Polydor
Soul Dressing...................................Stax

## SOLOMON BURKE
The Best of Solomon Burke.....................Atlantic
Greatest Hits.................................Atlantic

## ARETHA FRANKLIN
Aretha Arrives................................Atlantic
Aretha's Gold.................................Atlantic
Aretha's Greatest Hits........................Atlantic
Aretha in Paris...............................Atlantic
Aretha Franklin's Greatest Hits...............Columbia
Aretha Franklin Soul '69......................Atlantic
Aretha Lady Soul..............................Atlantic
I Never Loved A Man...........................Atlantic
Ten Years of Gold.............................Atlantic
Young, Gifted and Black.......................Atlantic

## JIMI HENDRIX

Are You Experienced? ...........................Reprise
Axis: Bold As Love...............................Reprise
Electric Ladyland ...............................Reprise
Hendrix Band of Gypsies with Buddy Miles and Billy Cox
Capitol
Rare Hendrix ......................................Trip
Smash Hits.......................................Reprise
Soundtrack Recordings from the film *Jimi Hendrix* .....Reprise

## ISLEY BROTHERS

The Best of the Isley Brothers.......................Buddah
Greatest Hits....................................T Neck
It's Our Thing....................................T Neck
Shout..............................................RCA
This Old Heart of Mine ...........................Tamla
Twist and Shout ..................................Wand
Very Best of.........................................UA

## WILSON PICKETT

The Best of Wilson Pickett—Volumes I and II .........Atlantic
Great Hits.........................................Wand
Hey Jude..........................................Atlantic
If You Need Me....................................Atlantic
I'm in Love ......................................Atlantic
In Philadelphia ..................................Atlantic
In the Midnight Hour .............................Atlantic
Midnight Mover ..................................Atlantic
Right On ..........................................Atlantic

## OTIS REDDING

Dictionary of Soul ...............................Atlantic
Dock of the Bay ..................................Atlantic
History of Otis Redding ..........................Atlantic
Immortal Otis Redding ...........................Atlantic
King and Queen with Carla Thomas ...................Stax
Live in Europe....................................Atlantic
Love Man .........................................Atlantic
The Pain in My Heart .............................Atlantic

## THE ROLLING STONES

Aftermath......................................... London
Beggars Banquet .................................. London
Big Hits (High Tide and Green Grass)................. London
December's Children (And Everybody) ................ London
Exile on Main Street ......................... Rolling Stone
Get Yer Ya Ya's Out.............................. London
Hot Rocks—1964–1971........................... London
Let It Bleed..................................... London
Out of Our Heads ................................ London
The Rolling Stones ............................... London
The Rolling Stones Now........................... London
Sticky Fingers............................. Rolling Stone
12 X 15 ........................................ London

## SAM AND DAVE

Best of Sam and Dave ........................... Atlantic
Hold On I'm Comin' .............................. Stax
Sam and Dave .................................. Roulette
Soul Men ........................................ Stax

## PERCY SLEDGE

Take Time to Know Her........................... Atlantic
The Best of Percy Sledge......................... Atlantic
When a Man Loves a Woman ..................... Atlantic

## SLY AND THE FAMILY STONE

Dance to the Music................................. Epic
Greatest Hits ....................................... Epic
Life................................................ Epic
Stand.............................................. Epic
There's a Riot Going On............................. Epic
Whole New Thing ................................... Epic

# CHAPTER 9

# THE SEVENTIES

## A Mixed Bag

*Trouble is spreading, God knows where we're heading*

—Marvin Gaye

Writer Tom Wolfe called it "The Me Decade," a time when people stopped thinking about anything or anyone but themselves. In the sixties, there had been a lot of talk about the brotherhood of man. Now they were saying, "Get yours while you can."

There was a loss of faith and innocence in the seventies, and you could hear it in the music. "Too much war and too much public crime has poisoned the country to be easily put to rest by any kind of reform or vengeance," Greil Marcus writes in *Mystery Train*. "There is simply too much to forget:

> Our politics have robbed the good words of ethics of their meaning. . . . What, in the sixties, looked like a chance to find new forms of political life, has been replaced by a flight to privacy and cynicism. . . .

With race riots, Vietnam, and Watergate in the air, you couldn't expect very happy music. A few white performers like Van Morrison and the Band

Isaac Hayes, Van Morrison,
the O'Jays, Grace Jones.

tried to make optimistic music within the rhythm and blues tradition, but many black recording artists—taking their cue from Sly's *Riot* album—became introspective and even a little paranoid.

Marvin Gaye asked a lot of troubling questions on his song and album *What's Goin' On?* As the writer/artist/producer of Motown's first real concept album, Gaye was at the very pulse of the black experience in early-seventies America. "Makes me wanna holler, the way they do my life," Marvin Gaye cries in *Inner City Blues,* and he wasn't the only one who felt that way.

The *they* that Marvin was referring to was the same establishment whose "trigger-happy policemen" shot his brothers during urban race riots. *They* were the same "fathers" who were ruining the ecology and sending people (including many blacks) to die in a war that a majority of Americans had decided was wrong.

Other black recording artists may have been less explicitly social in their complaints, but their messages were just as disconcerting. "I wish somebody'd take some of these knives outta my back!" the O'Jays sang in "Back Stabbers." "Smiling faces sometimes tell lies," warned the Undisputed Truth. These bad feelings didn't just come out of a vacuum or even a couple of bad experiences.

"The world is a ghetto" sang the group War. And when you live in a ghetto, it's bound to take its toll. "You've been slippin' into darkness," War sang in their other hit. "Pretty soon you're gonna pay." The "darkness" that War was talking about was the result of drugs—a growing problem in the ghetto and elsewhere.

The so-called drug culture of the sixties was an important feature of such hippie strongholds as San Francisco's Haight-Ashbury. But it had been part of life in the black ghetto for decades. There never was much of a fuss made about drug abuse when it was just blacks doing it. But when white kids started dropping out and overdosing in the sixties, drug abuse became a national media issue.

Some blacks thought that drugs, like long hair, was a passing fad for young white kids. When many leaders of the sixties' hippie movement started cutting their hair and becoming politicians and stockbrokers, it didn't take long for blacks to figure out that they now stood pretty much alone.

Curtis Mayfield, the producer and lead singer of a Chicago-based vocal group called the Impressions, once wrote a song that asked: "If you had your choice of colors, which one would you choose my brother?" Black people didn't necessarily choose to be different or to stand out from the crowd. It simply came with the territory. This simple awareness changed the tone of rhythm and blues in the seventies from one that was universal, to one directed at the concerns of the ghetto.

"Respect Yourself," sang the Staples Singers. "Stay in School," sang James Brown. Curtis Mayfield was even more explicit in the soundtrack he wrote for the movie *Superfly*. "Another junkie plan," he sang in the song "Freddie's Dead," "pushin' dope for the man." *The man* Mayfield was singing about was organized crime. But when you came right down to it, these drug suppliers weren't that far removed from the establishment figures Marvin Gaye referred to as *they* in "What's Goin' On?" When all was said and done, the cops, the mob, and the politicians all seemed to be part of the same corruption and racism. "If we're going to rise above all this adversity," rhythm and blues songs seemed to be saying, "we're going to have to do it by ourselves."

After Marvin Gaye's *What's Goin' On?* album became a huge commercial success, Motown became a contributor to this early-seventies voice. The Berry Gordy–produced film, *Lady Sings the Blues* with Diana Ross, graphically diagrammed both the pains of growing up black in a poor and broken home and the murderous effects of heroin. But it was a song by the Temptations called "Papa Was a Rolling Stone" that provided both the most searing exploration of the black experience and the most creative use of rhythm and blues.

"Papa Was a Rolling Stone" was, among many other things, a ten-minute-long jazz piece that owed its instrumental flavor to *In a Silent Way* and *Bitches Brew,* two jazz fusion albums by Miles Davis. The singing was pure Family Stone, with the entire group taking turns telling the story of four children asking their mother what kind of a man their recently deceased father was.

"Hey mama," one son implores his mother, "is it true what they say, that papa never worked a day in his life?" The mother can only shake her head and answer: "Papa was a rolling stone . . . and when he died, all he left us was alone."

After this classic record became a huge hit, Motown released a series of inferior sound-alikes, and eventually abandoned the socially concerned approach altogether. This seemed to mirror the sentiments of many black people, who really didn't want to dwell that much on the problems of the ghetto. If it was going to be a matter of sink or swim, the smart move was to get your act together and get your butt out of the ghetto completely. This seemed like a good tack in the seventies, but for some ambitious black people, the desire to make it in the white man's world also meant discarding any and all music that was associated with the ghetto.

"Even now," says Bobby Robinson, "many upwardly mobile blacks don't want to know from blues, gospel, or straight-ahead rhythm and blues."

Doc Pomus has noticed pretty much the same phenomenon during the past ten years or so. "It's interesting how things have changed," he remarks.

> Before the sixties, when you went to a blues show, you hardly ever saw white people. Now when you go to a blues show, you don't see very many black people. For some reason, a lot of black people don't relate to the blues anymore. They want to live in suburbia, listen to disco music, and pick up on all the problems that white people have.

Record producers are ever astute in keeping up with changing attitudes and a changing market. If black people wanted upwardly mobile music, then upwardly mobile music they would get. A variety of technological improvements that were introduced in the seventies helped rhythm and blues producers to achieve this end.

The Beatles and Otis Redding had recorded their best work on four-track recorders. In the early seventies, sixteen tracks became a music industry standard. This meant that it was now possible to better separate and manipulate the sounds of various instrumental and vocal parts. These technical manipulations allowed producers to make records that were far cleaner and slicker than in the past. But instead of using these innovations simply to facilitate the recording process, more and more producers were centering their music around this super-clean, upwardly mobile techno-sound.

There were some terrific soul-influenced records in the early seventies that used the improved recording technologies to good effect. In Philadelphia, the Gamble and Huff production team scored a huge crossover hit with the O'Jays' "Love Train." Thom Bell, another Philadelphia producer, had success with the Spinners, a former Motown group. On Spinners records like "I'll Be Around" and "Could it Be I'm Falling in Love," Bell used a prominent bass line grounded with a sizzling drum figure that would resurface a few years later as "the disco beat."

In Memphis, producer Willie Mitchell used a similar rhythmic style with Al Green—a singer who seemed to have absorbed and expanded on Otis Redding's vocal style. On hits like "Let's Stay Together," "Tired of Being Alone," and "You Ought to Be with Me," Green and Mitchell successfully combined a sixties soul sensibility with a clean, slick seventies feel. Unfortunately, Al Green never achieved the kind of stardom his talent seemed to warrant. What might have been even more unfortunate, though, is that other producers who copied Mitchell's technical innovations pretty much ignored his soul influences.

The Spinners—scored big with the Philadelphia sound.

*Disco Remembered*

They don't talk about it that much anymore, but for a few years in the seventies, disco became both the dominant form of popular music and a style that some people loved to hate. From one point of view, disco was no great departure as music. Neither was it that big a deal as a social phenomenon. We had, after all, gone through something quite similar in the previous decade.

The strong dance beat has always been an important part of rhythm and blues. In the early sixties, an unknown singer named Chubby Checker had a huge hit with a remake of a Hank Ballard song called "The Twist." Suddenly, a new dance craze was born. Inter-

estingly, so-called twist music had the identical beat of
other rhythm and blues of that era. But for some
reason, people who had previously expressed a
strong dislike for rhythm and blues and rock 'n' roll
were taking twist lessons and lining up at the hundreds of twist clubs—called discotheques—that were
springing up all over America.

New York's Peppermint Lounge was the most famous discotheque during the twist craze. Celebrities
like the Duke of Bedford and former two-time Demo-
cratic presidential candidate Adlai Stevenson were
standing in line to dance to the music of the Peppermint Lounge's house band, Joey Dee and the Star-
lighters. Some younger rhythm and blues listeners
found these events troubling. How could they be expected to take this music seriously when their parents—and even grandparents—were suddenly dancing to it?

In many respects, the coming of disco paralleled
the Twist craze of the previous decade. At first, it
didn't seem like any kind of great departure. Audiences were in a dancing mood in the early seventies
and they were interested in what critic Vince Aletti
called "party music." Dancers in black and gay clubs
had a particular preference for long, dramatic records with a prominent drum beat. In 1973, Aletti
cited Motown and the music of Sly Stone and Issac
Hayes as the immediate forerunners of party music.
This music started to develop a life of its own when
music industry insiders began to notice that certain
records were selling solely on the basis of their popularity in dance halls.

In 1974, Manu Dibango's "Soul Makossa," a

French import with an African feel, became the first dance club hit to also become a radio hit. By the following year, a number of other records had repeated the same club-hit-to-radio-hit pattern. These included "Love's Theme" by Barry White's Love Unlimited Orchestra, the Hues Corporation's "Rock the Boat," and George McCrae's "Rock Your Baby" and "The Hustle" by Van McCoy.

Here again, this "new" music wasn't altogether that new, even if its spirit was being shaped by a previously overlooked source. This is how *Rolling Stone's* Stephen Holden described the small group of disco disc jockeys, who were actually creating hits on their own:

> A potent new breed of media maven . . . a prime mover in the development of disco: . . . The club DJ's prided themselves on psyching out a crowd and then programming them into an ecstatic frenzy, slip-cuing records into a continuous sequence and equalizing them for dancing by boosting the bass. The top DJ's became taste-making alchemists-engineers with cults that followed them from club to club. . . . [They were] the largely unsung pioneers of . . . disco.

Once the record industry began to fully understand how important these DJ's could be in breaking a record, they began to gear their product to the needs of club dancers. Neil Bogart of Casablanca Records was one of the first record executives to jump on the disco bandwagon. When an unknown European record producer named Giorgio Moroder approached Bogart with a three-minute version of "Love to Love You Baby" by an equally unknown singer named Donna Summer, Bogart asked Moroder to expand the song to sixteen minutes. The first disco record to take up an entire album side, "Love to Love You Baby" became a massive club and radio hit.

Although Donna Summer was to become disco's most prominent sex symbol, she soon proved that she was a talented singer who didn't depend on the disco format to score hits. But as the popularity of disco grew, it managed to swallow up almost every kind of performer and every musical style in its wake. By the late seventies, everyone from Tina Turner to Ethel Merman to Donald Duck had made a disco record.

As a musical style, disco absorbed rhythm and blues, rock and roll, jazz, the samba, and even classical music. For a while there, almost every record you heard was either disco or disco-influenced. Bobby Robinson was one of many knowledgeable observers who felt that disco was having a negative effect on rhythm and blues and other authentic forms.

> I felt the strong impact of disco put all the rhythm and blues artists on hold for a number of years. The music was sort of sidetracked by the strong impact of the disco thing. It just sort of wiped everything out. There was nothing happening with real rhythm and blues. It was just disco, disco, disco. But finally, it just kind of burned itself out. People got tired of disco because it was more or less the same thing over and over again.

A few interesting events took place before disco burned itself out as *the* pop phenomenon. The 1977 movie *Saturday Night Fever* introduced a new kind of disco and a new kind of disco hero. The phenomenally popular soundtrack that the Bee Gees wrote for that film had a standard disco beat (125–134 beats per minute). But the songs were strong and catchy

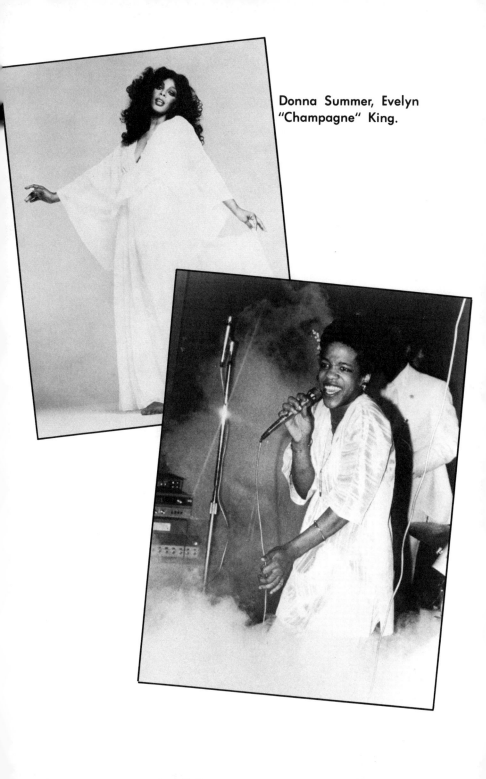

Donna Summer, Evelyn "Champagne" King.

A Taste of Honey.

The Bee Gees,
Rod Stewart.

Blondie's Deborah Harry.

enough to earn the praise of a number of hardcore disco haters. Furthermore, as a working-class kid from Brooklyn who lived for the dance floor, John Travolta's Tony Manero seemed like the kind of guy who would crave rock and roll, not disco. But by the late seventies, the beat of most danceable rock and roll had taken on the disco beat.

Many rock fans and critics bristled when some of their favorites came out with disco records. And, in fact, a lot of that stuff was garbage, nothing more than an attempt to capitalize on a current fad. But some rock artists managed to make good records while utilizing a disco beat. The Rolling Stones' "Miss

You," Rod Stewart's "Do Ya Think I'm Sexy" and Blondie's "Heart of Glass" were good pop records by any standards. These three rock artists, along with the Bee Gees and Donna Summer, proved that the disco beat and rock were indeed compatible.

There never was any kind of official end to the disco craze. The music is still very popular in the clubs that spawned it. If you turn on a rhythm and blues radio station, you are still likely to hear a good many songs that would fit the requirements of seventies disco. The prominent dance beat, extra-long renditions of songs, and super-clean, high-tech recording quality have left their mark on both rhythm and blues and rock. Yes, disco is still with us, but at least Donald Duck has stopped making dance records. Thank goodness for small favors!

*Reggae*

The sound of Jamaica continues to leave its mark on today's rhythm and blues and rock. *Rolling Stone*'s Jim Miller once called reggae "the most vital adaptation of rhythm and blues since the early days of the Rolling Stones." Unfortunately, a comprehensive discussion of reggae and the social conditions that gave rise to the music are beyond the scope of this book. Still, Jamaican music has become so important that some mention of it must be included in a discussion of contemporary rhythm and blues.

In the early seventies, American recording artists began recording some of their work in Jamaica. Paul Simon's "Mother and Child Reunion" and Johnny Nash's "I Can See Clearly Now" were two reggae-tinged hits of that era. During that same period, a film called *The Harder They Come,* starring Jimmy Cliff, became an underground hit.

The film touched on some of the social struggles that are still going on in Jamaica, as seen through the eyes of an aspiring reggae singer. The soundtrack to *The Harder They Come* established Cliff as a strong rhythm and blues singer. It also featured songs by another group, Toots and the Maytals, whose lead singer was strongly influenced by Otis Redding.

The world that American viewers were introduced to in *The Harder They Come* was a major theme of the reggae artist who has had the greatest impact on today's music. American listeners were introduced to Bob Marley's music through Eric Clapton's "I Shot the Sheriff" and Johnny Nash's "Stir It Up." But in the next few years, Bob Marley would establish himself as the outstanding new rhythm and blues artist of the seventies. The son of a Jamaican woman and an English sea captain, Marley became an international star during the last years of his life. Though his influence is pervasive, Marley's own records have only recently begun attracting American listeners.

Bob Marley's importance lies not only in his considerable talents as a singer, songwriter, and band leader, but also in his roots in authentic rhythm and blues styles. When you listen to Marley's records, you can hear that he grew up with American rhythm and blues. But Marley's roots go well beyond a familiarity with the records of such great black American artists as James Brown, Otis Redding, and the Impressions. When Bobby Robinson listens to a Bob Marley record, he is struck by the heritage Jamaican blacks share with their American counterparts.

Bob Marley (front) with the original Wailers—the most influential performer of the late '70s.

When the slave ships used to go up the gold coast of Africa and bring back two hundred slaves, they'd leave half in the West Indies and take the rest to the South—to ports like Charleston, South Carolina. But it was the same people with the same roots. . . . Even though Bob Marley picked up rhythm and blues from the radio, he felt that link in his past with his ancestors who got off the boat in Charleston. The music he makes varied that calypso rhythm, emphasizing the "off" part of the beat, and used the things he liked in rhythm and blues.

Though Bob Marley is still not all that well recognized in America, he remains one of the few popular artists with that special ability to bring diverse audiences and musical styles together. Like Sly Stone in the sixties, Marley had the uncanny knack of using everything at his disposal. This included the music and his life experience as a half-black Jamaican. It also included the sounds he heard and loved while he was growing up.

Marley was moved by the great rhythm and blues artists. But he was also affected by rock artists like Bob Dylan and jazz artists like Miles Davis and Lester Young. It takes a rare talent to absorb all those sounds and find a way of synthesizing them into an original musical statement. It takes an even rarer talent to deliver a spiritual message to an international following. That is what Bob Marley accomplished in his short life.

In a *Musician* article called "Reggae '84," writer Roger Steffans described Bob Marley's lasting importance this way:

> Bob was not in music to make money. Marley's hopes and ears were tuned to Eternity . . . [He wanted to share] his messages . . . with the world. And how the world responded! From Tokyo to Aukland, from New York to Soweto, the words and works of Bob Marley were studied, sung, debated, dissected, and sloganized, uniting black, brown, red, yellow, and white in one common understanding. But why? It was because Bob Marley, with his half-white heritage and personal agenda, symbolized a bold cultural bridge . . . forging a dynamic bond between old sorrows and new struggles. More than virtually any other figure on the American scene, Marley was the inspirational voice of self-determination.

Flawed, troubled, yet generous and committed, he was also its heroic embodiment. You can't say that about a David Bowie or a Prince.

## Rap: The sound of the ghetto

As the seventies ended, a new kind of music called *rap* emerged from the ghetto streets. In a sense, rap was the most original black folk form to emerge in years, because, like blues and gospel music, it was an actual expression of what black people were feeling. The people in this case, though, were not itinerant laborers or church worshipers. They were teenage boys who were, more often than not, members of neighborhood gangs.

Bobby Robinson, as a resident of Harlem, had heard kids rapping for a number of years. But for a while, he did not think that this street phenomenon would surface as a commercial rhythm and blues style.

> The very first rap record hit the streets in September of '79. That was "Sugar Hill Delight" by the Sugarhill Gang. It had been around the streets for a year or two before that. Outdoors in the park and the street parties in the summer, kids at the PAL centers. I heard it all around but I didn't bother with it. But when this Sugar Hill thing became such a tremendous smash, I said, "This thing's been under my nose for the past two, three years with these kids right out on the street." So I put it out on the grapevine that I was looking for the best rap acts. Right away, I got called by the Funky Four out of the Bronx—a dynamite little group—and we put out an instant rap hit.

Though it took Bobby some time to recognize the commercial potential of rap, he immediately understood the forces that gave rise to the music. "Rap came on the heels of the riots," he recalls, "and a general period of social turbulence. The kids who came out of that social revolution were a highly charged bunch, psychologically, because that's the kind of era they came out of."

Bobby also thinks it's significant that rap started in the South Bronx—one of the worst ghettos in America. "Parts of that neighborhood looked like bombed-out Berlin. A lot of the kids who lived there had televisions or watched television at a friend's house. They watched the good life and saw all of the things that they didn't have, and their imagination soared."

In essence, rap was an expression of restlessness and defiance. Many of the best rappers were gang kids and their messages were geared to let you know how macho they were. "All of the early raps were basically along the same lines," Bobby Robinson recalls. "They were all kind of like this:"

*We're goin' to the top*
*We ain't gonna stop*
*And we're the ones.*
*I can rap you all night*
*Gonna rock you all night . . .*

Within a few short years, this neighborhood phenomenon that had started at summer block parties and playgrounds had emerged as a commercial rhythm and blues form. One reason for the popularity of rap was that it was, at first anyway, strictly a black-ghetto product. Also, because it didn't require any particular singing talent, rap was something that almost anyone could do. With the advent of synthesizers and computerized drum machines, it became possible to make a rap record virtually without any musicians. But Bobby Robinson insists that not everyone has what it takes to be a good rapper:

> Rapping is not singing, but it does require talent. A good rapper is fast-thinking and has the ability to speak with certain rhythmic inflections. You need a rapid-fire delivery. And you have to slur words, and then cut them short. It's almost like a musical instrument. You have to know how to inflect—to make the words have a certain meaning with certain impact. You also have to know when to back off and when to push hard.

Because Bobby Robinson was so well-respected as a rhythm and blues producer, many of the best rappers answered his call for new groups. After his success with the Funky Four, Bobby had rap hits with

**Parliament, rap and funk pioneers.**

202 / THE RHYTHM AND BLUES STORY

groups like Kool Kyle the Star Child, Dr. Ice, the Disco Four, the Fearless Four, and a Spanish rap group called Spanish Fly. But Robinson's best-known rap hit was "Super Rappin'" by Grand Master Flash, who, along with Curtis Blow, is still the most popular rap act worldwide.

Like many rhythm and blues forms, the rap attracts a bigger following in Europe than in the United States. But recently, it has found new life among a growing number of American listeners. Break Dancing has kept the rap at the forefront of today's music. Also, rock artists like Peter Wolf are currently introducing rap and black funk to a whole new audience. It's hard to say if this cross-pollenization will lead to the kind of musical togetherness that seemed to be in the wind during the sixties. But at this time, the emerging picture looks far more promising than it has for some time.

## SEVENTIES SELECTED DISCOGRAPHY

**BEE GEES**

The Bee Gees' Greatest Hits . . . . . . . . . . . . . . . . . . . . . . . . . RSO
Saturday Night Fever . . . . . . . . . . . . . . . . . . . . . . . . . . . RSO
Spirits Having Flown. . . . . . . . . . . . . . . . . . . . . . . . . . . . RSO

**BLONDIE**

AutoAmerica. . . . . . . . . . . . . . . . . . . . . . . . . . . . . . . Chrysalis
The Best of Blondie. . . . . . . . . . . . . . . . . . . . . . . . . . . Chrysalis
Blondie Private Stock . . . . . . . . . . . . . . . . . . . . . . . . . Chrysalis
Eat to the Beat . . . . . . . . . . . . . . . . . . . . . . . . . . . . . Chrysalis
The Hunter . . . . . . . . . . . . . . . . . . . . . . . . . . . . . . . Chrysalis
Koo-Koo (Debbie Harry solo) . . . . . . . . . . . . . . . . . . . . Chrysalis
Parallel Lines. . . . . . . . . . . . . . . . . . . . . . . . . . . . . . Chrysalis
Plastic Letters . . . . . . . . . . . . . . . . . . . . . . . . . . . . . Chrysalis

## KURTIS BLOW
Kurtis Blow . . . . . . . . . . . . . . . . . . . . . . . . . . . . Mercury/Polygram

## ERIC CLAPTON
Backless. . . . . . . . . . . . . . . . . . . . . . . . . . . . . . . . . . . . . . RSO
The Best of Eric Clapton . . . . . . . . . . . . . . . . . . . . . . . . . RSO
No Reason to Cry . . . . . . . . . . . . . . . . . . . . . . . . . . . . . . . RSO
Slow Hand . . . . . . . . . . . . . . . . . . . . . . . . . . . . . . . . . . . . RSO

## JIMMY CLIFF
Can't Get Enough . . . . . . . . . . . . . . . . . . . . . . . . . . . . . . Veep
The Harder They Come (Soundtrack) . . . . . . . . . . . . . . . . Island
Special . . . . . . . . . . . . . . . . . . . . . . . . . . . . . . . . . . . Columbia
Wonderful World. . . . . . . . . . . . . . . . . . . . . . . . . . . . . A & M

## MANU DIBANGO
Afrovision. . . . . . . . . . . . . . . . . . . . . . . . . . . . . . . . . . Island

## GRAND MASTER FLASH
The Message. . . . . . . . . . . . . . . . . . . . . . . . . . . . . . . Sugarhill

## AL GREEN
Al Green Is Love. . . . . . . . . . . . . . . . . . . . . . . . . . . . . . . HI
Back Up Train . . . . . . . . . . . . . . . . . . . . . . . . . . . . . . Action
Belle Album . . . . . . . . . . . . . . . . . . . . . . . . . . . . . . . . . . HI
Call Me. . . . . . . . . . . . . . . . . . . . . . . . . . . . . . . . . . . . . HI
Cream of Al Green. . . . . . . . . . . . . . . . . . . . . . . . . . . Cream
Explores Your Mind . . . . . . . . . . . . . . . . . . . . . . . . . . . . HI
Full of Fire . . . . . . . . . . . . . . . . . . . . . . . . . . . . . . . . . . . HI
Gets Next to You . . . . . . . . . . . . . . . . . . . . . . . . . . . . . . HI
Green Is Blues . . . . . . . . . . . . . . . . . . . . . . . . . . . . . . . . HI
Have a Good Time. . . . . . . . . . . . . . . . . . . . . . . . . . . . . HI
I'm Still in Love with You. . . . . . . . . . . . . . . . . . . . . . . . HI
Let's Stay Together . . . . . . . . . . . . . . . . . . . . . . . . . . . . HI
Living for You. . . . . . . . . . . . . . . . . . . . . . . . . . . . . . . . . HI
Truth and Time . . . . . . . . . . . . . . . . . . . . . . . . . . . . . . . HI

## ISAAC HAYES
And Once Again . . . . . . . . . . . . . . . . . . . . . . . . . . . Polydor
The Isaac Hayes Movement . . . . . . . . . . . . . . . . . . . . . Stax

## IMPRESSIONS

The Best of the Impressions . . . . . . . . . . . . . . . . . . . . . . . . . . ABC
Collection . . . . . . . . . . . . . . . . . . . . . . . . . . . . . . . . . . . . . . . . ABC
Come to My Party . . . . . . . . . . . . . . . . . . . . . . . . . . . . . Chi-Soung
The Fabulous Impressions . . . . . . . . . . . . . . . . . . . . . . . . . . . ABC
The Impressions' Greatest Hits . . . . . . . . . . . . . . . . . . . . . . . ABC
The Impressions: The Vintage Years . . . . . . . . . . . . . . . . . . . ABC
Keep on Pushing . . . . . . . . . . . . . . . . . . . . . . . . . . . . . . . . . . . ABC
The Never-Ending Impressions . . . . . . . . . . . . . . . . . . . . . . . ABC
One by One . . . . . . . . . . . . . . . . . . . . . . . . . . . . . . . . . . . . . . . ABC
People Get Ready . . . . . . . . . . . . . . . . . . . . . . . . . . . . . . . . . . ABC
Ridin' High . . . . . . . . . . . . . . . . . . . . . . . . . . . . . . . . . . . . . . . . ABC
We're a Winner . . . . . . . . . . . . . . . . . . . . . . . . . . . . . . . . . . . . ABC

## BOB MARLEY AND THE WAILERS

Babylon by Bus . . . . . . . . . . . . . . . . . . . . . . . . . . . . . . . . . . Island
Birth of a Legend . . . . . . . . . . . . . . . . . . . . . . . . . . . . . . . . . . Epic
Burning . . . . . . . . . . . . . . . . . . . . . . . . . . . . . . . . . . . . . . . . Island
Catch a Fire . . . . . . . . . . . . . . . . . . . . . . . . . . . . . . . . . . . . Island
Exodus . . . . . . . . . . . . . . . . . . . . . . . . . . . . . . . . . . . . . . . . Island
In the Beginning . . . . . . . . . . . . . . . . . . . . . . . . . . . . . . . . Psycho
Jah Live . . . . . . . . . . . . . . . . . . . . . . . . . . . . . . . . . . . . . . . Island
Kaya . . . . . . . . . . . . . . . . . . . . . . . . . . . . . . . . . . . . . . . . . . Island
Live . . . . . . . . . . . . . . . . . . . . . . . . . . . . . . . . . . . . . . . . . . . Island
Natty Dread . . . . . . . . . . . . . . . . . . . . . . . . . . . . . . . . . . . . Island
Survival . . . . . . . . . . . . . . . . . . . . . . . . . . . . . . . . . . . . . . . Island
Uprising . . . . . . . . . . . . . . . . . . . . . . . . . . . . . . . . . . . . . . . Island

## CURTIS MAYFIELD

America Today . . . . . . . . . . . . . . . . . . . . . . . . . . . . . . . . . Curtom
Back to the World . . . . . . . . . . . . . . . . . . . . . . . . . . . . . . Buddah
Do It All Night . . . . . . . . . . . . . . . . . . . . . . . . . . . . . . . . . Curtom
Got to Find a Way . . . . . . . . . . . . . . . . . . . . . . . . . . . . . . Curtom
Heartbeat . . . . . . . . . . . . . . . . . . . . . . . . . . . . . . . . . . . . . Curtom
Love Is the Place . . . . . . . . . . . . . . . . . . . . . . . . . . . . Boardwalk
Move on Up . . . . . . . . . . . . . . . . . . . . . . . . . . . . . . . . . . Buddah
Something to Believe In . . . . . . . . . . . . . . . . . . . . . . . . . . . . RSO
Short Eyes . . . . . . . . . . . . . . . . . . . . . . . . . . . . . . . . . . . . Curtom
Superfly . . . . . . . . . . . . . . . . . . . . . . . . . . . . . . . . . . . . . . Buddah
Roots . . . . . . . . . . . . . . . . . . . . . . . . . . . . . . . . . . . . . . . . Curtom

## VAN MORRISON

Astral Weeks............................ Warner Brothers
Beautiful Vision.......................... Warner Brothers
Best of Van Morrison .............................. Bang
Common One................................... Mercury
Hard Nose the Highway................... Warner Brothers
His Band and Street Choir ................ Warner Brothers
Into the Music ................................ Mercury
Moondance.............................. Warner Brothers
Period of Transition...................... Warner Brothers
St. Dominics Preview .................... Warner Brothers
Veedon Fleece........................... Warner Brothers
Wavelength............................. Warner Brothers
Sense of Wonder ............................. Polygram

## THE O'JAYS

Back Stabbers............................. Philadelphia
Family Reunion............................ Philadelphia
Greatest Hits............................. Philadelphia
Identify Yourself .......................... Philadelphia
In Philaderlphia .......................... Philadelphia
My Favorite Person........................ Philadelphia
Message in the Music ..................... Philadelphia
So Full of Love ........................... Philadelphia
Survival.................................. Philadelphia
The Year 2000............................ Philadelphia
Travelin' at the Speed of Light ............. Philadelphia

## PAUL SIMON

Greatest Hits Etc..................................... CBS
Mother and Child Reunion .......................... CBS
Still Crazy after All These Years ...................... CBS
There Goes Rhymin' Simon.......................... CBS

## THE SPINNERS

Can't Shake This Feeling......................... Atlantic
Dancin' and Lovin' .............................. Atlantic
Love Trippin' .................................. Atlantic

## THE STAPLES SINGERS

*I'll Take You There* . . . . . . . . . . . . . . . . . . . . . . . . . . . . . . . . . . . Stax
*Respect Yourself* . . . . . . . . . . . . . . . . . . . . . . . . . . . . . . . . . . . . Stax

## ROD STEWART

*Absolutely Free* . . . . . . . . . . . . . . . . . . . . . . . . . . . Warner Brothers
*Best of—Volumes I and II* . . . . . . . . . . . . . . . . . . . . . . . Mercury
*Blonds Have More Fun* . . . . . . . . . . . . . . . . . . . Warner Brothers
*Body Wishes* . . . . . . . . . . . . . . . . . . . . . . . . . . . . Warner Brothers
*Camouflage* . . . . . . . . . . . . . . . . . . . . . . . . . . . Warner Brothers
*Every Picture Tells a Story* . . . . . . . . . . . . . . . . . . Warner Brothers
*Greatest Hits* . . . . . . . . . . . . . . . . . . . . . . . . . . . Warner Brothers
*Tonight I'm Yours* . . . . . . . . . . . . . . . . . . . . . . . Warner Brothers
*Vintage Years 69/70* . . . . . . . . . . . . . . . . . . . . . . . . . . . . Mercury

## SUGARHILL GANG

*8th Wonder* . . . . . . . . . . . . . . . . . . . . . . . . . . . . . . . . . . . . Sugarhill
*Rapper's Delight* . . . . . . . . . . . . . . . . . . . . . . . . . . . . . . . Sugarhill
*The Sugarhill Gang* . . . . . . . . . . . . . . . . . . . . . . . . . . . . . Sugarhill

## DONNA SUMMER

*A Love Trilogy* . . . . . . . . . . . . . . . . . . . . . . . . . . . . . . Casablanca
*Bad Girls* . . . . . . . . . . . . . . . . . . . . . . . . . . . . . . . . . . Casablanca
*Four Seasons of Love* . . . . . . . . . . . . . . . . . . . . . . . . . Casablanca
*I Remember Yesterday* . . . . . . . . . . . . . . . . . . . . . . . . Casablanca
*Live and More* . . . . . . . . . . . . . . . . . . . . . . . . . . . . . . Casablanca
*Love to Love You Baby* . . . . . . . . . . . . . . . . . . . . . . . Casablanca
*Once Upon a Time* . . . . . . . . . . . . . . . . . . . . . . . . . . Casablanca
*On the Radio—Greatest Hits, Volumes I & II* . . . . . . . Casablanca
*She Works Hard for the Money* . . . . . . . . . . . . . . . . . . . Mercury
*Donna Summer* . . . . . . . . . . . . . . . . . . . . . . . . . . . . . . . Geffen
*The Wanderer* . . . . . . . . . . . . . . . . . . . . . . . . . . Geffen/Warner

## THE UNDISPUTED TRUTH

*The Best of the Undisputed Truth* . . . . . . . . . . . . . . . . . . . Motown
*Cosmic Truth* . . . . . . . . . . . . . . . . . . . . . . . . . . . . . . . . . Motown
*Down to Earth* . . . . . . . . . . . . . . . . . . . . . . . . . . . . . . . . Motown
*Face to Face* . . . . . . . . . . . . . . . . . . . . . . . . . . . . . . . . . Motown
*Law of the Land* . . . . . . . . . . . . . . . . . . . . . . . . . . . . . . . Motown

*Method to the Madness* . . . . . . . . . . . . . . . . . . . . Warner Brothers
*Undisputed Truth*. . . . . . . . . . . . . . . . . . . . . . . . . . . . . . Motown

## WAR

*Greatest Hits* . . . . . . . . . . . . . . . . . . . . . . . . . . . United Artists
*Love Is* . . . . . . . . . . . . . . . . . . . . . . . . . . . . . . . United Artists
*The Music Band* . . . . . . . . . . . . . . . . . . . . . . . . . . . . . MCA
*Outlaw* . . . . . . . . . . . . . . . . . . . . . . . . . . . . . . . . . . . RCA
*Platinum* . . . . . . . . . . . . . . . . . . . . . . . . . . . . . . Blue Note
*War* . . . . . . . . . . . . . . . . . . . . . . . . . . . . . . . United Artists

## BARRY WHITE

*Beware*. . . . . . . . . . . . . . . . . . . . . . . . . . . . . Unlimited Gold
*Change*. . . . . . . . . . . . . . . . . . . . . . . . . . . . . Unlimited Gold
*The Man*. . . . . . . . . . . . . . . . . . . . . . . . . . . . . Unlimited Gold
*The Message Is Love* . . . . . . . . . . . . . . . . . . . . . Unlimited Gold
*Barry White's Sheet Music* . . . . . . . . . . . . . . . . . Unlimited Gold
*Under the Influence of . . . Love Unlimited*. . . . . . Love Unlimited

# CHAPTER 10

# GARY BONDS AND BRUCE SPRINGSTEEN

## Bringing the Past and Present Together

In the late fifties, Gary U.S. Bonds made a series of up-tempo records that were some of the best, high-spirited party music ever. One of these records, "A Quarter to Three," has long been a staple of Bruce Springsteen's live set. They say that every singer can trace his major influence back to a single record. Listen to Bruce sing "A Quarter to Three" and then compare it to Gary Bonds's original version. You'll soon discover the root of Bruce's overall vocal style.

One night, Bruce showed up at a small New Jersey club where Gary was singing. Before long, Gary invited Bruce to sit in. Springsteen was delighted to find that his idol sounded as good as ever. He felt that a performer with Gary's talent deserved a record deal and the opportunity to play concerts. But in the mind of the public, Gary Bonds was a has-been,

Bruce Springsteen—an exceptional person (on stage with Miami Steve).

a relic who had not had a hit for over twenty years. Though Gary had managed to make a comfortable living working oldies shows, clubs, and colleges, there were few who thought he was ever going to make the charts again. Gary himself had more or less given up hope of making any kind of a major comeback.

> After my last hit in the early sixties, I did a couple of one-shot deals with different companies. I wasn't really dedicated into doing what I wanted to do. I later did some stuff with Jerry Lee Lewis. That was totally ridiculous because the sound was bad and we were working on a cheap scale. But I was making a living in music. I never had to worry about waking up six, seven o'clock in the morning and going to a job.

Truthfully, Bruce has been the closest I've come to salvation in the last fifteen years. I was working with a little disco group in Jersey when Bruce came up to me. I had no idea who he was, but I was told that we had a celebrity in the audience and I asked if maybe he would come up and do a little number for us. And there he was—Bruce Springsteen. The place went wild. Everybody started rushing to see him. Soon, the place was a mess. He got up and he did "A Quarter to Three" with me. We had a good time, jamming for about a half hour.

Afterwards, we talked for a while and then met for lunch later on in the month. I asked him about producing me and he said he was just going to ask me the same thing. He said that he would love to record me. A few months later, it happened, and thank God good things are happening again for me, as far as the record business is concerned. This is far more interesting than what I was anticipating doing for the rest of my life.

Bruce had taken some lumps in his own career, and understood the realities of the music business. If Gary Bonds was to get another shot at the top, Bruce would have to lend his own name to the proceedings. To insure the success of the project, Bruce sang and coproduced on Gary's album *Dedication.* Naturally, it was a hit. Though it was a fine record on its own merits, few people would have cared or noticed it if the name of Bruce Springsteen hadn't been associated with the project.

Gary Bonds is well aware that the story of his comeback is rare indeed. He knows too many other talented performers from his era who still work funky clubs and oldies shows for peanuts. But Gary Bonds has paid too many dues to imagine that his future is guaranteed.

I was lucky [even back in the fifties]. A guy asked me to make a record. I said yes and there I was. Today, for someone who wants to break into the business it's still a question of who you know. . . . When you walk into a record company, you've got to convince the guy behind the desk that this is a hit record. Even if you get in to someone in a power position you've got to convince him that it's good, and even if he thinks it's good he may not put it out because it's not what he's looking for this week. In this business, it's often more important to be lucky than good.

Gary's luck has proven to be exceptional. Lots of rock stars pay lip service to their gratitude to the older performers who laid the groundwork, but few take any real steps to help them. These debts are, of course, questions of personal choice. The fact is, though, that without Robert Johnson, there would be no Eric Clapton. Without Big Momma Thornton, there never would have been a Janis Joplin. If there had never been a Lloyd Price or a Little Richard, John Lennon and Paul McCartney would have had no firm starting point for their singing. And the list goes on and on.

When a white rock star makes it a point to resurrect the career of an older black musician who influenced him, it lends encouragement to other great performers who are toiling in small clubs and oldies shows, without any real prospects of landing a major record deal. Gary Bonds is a gifted musical artist, but without Bruce Springsteen, he would probably still be considered just another pleasant memory from a bygone era. Yet Gary Bonds is only one of many older performers who could still electrify today's audiences if given half a chance.

**Gary Bonds in the early '60s—"I was lucky."**

Bruce Springsteen is, as most of his fans know, an exceptional person. He is one of the very few superstars who maintains a real connection with both the audiences who support him and the older artists who nurtured him. Bruce realizes that rhythm and blues and rock 'n' roll are more than just names on some radio station manager's format sheet or categories on some record company executive's roster. He understands how hard it is to keep a career going once you've been labeled over-the-hill or uncommercial by the record industry. In the final analysis, though, there is little even someone as concerned and powerful as Bruce Springsteen can do to change the overall situation.

Unfortunately, exploitation and human suffering of one kind or another have always played a major role in the rhythm and blues story. It is truly sad that so many of the great artists who created this music are victims of a cold business interested only in how many copies a performer's last record sold. How different our story would be if only there were more Tina Turners whose careers exploded after years of scuffling, or more Bruce Springsteens who took the time and trouble to revive the fortunes of a Gary Bonds. But, as we've seen, this music has always been about the ability to laugh, to party, and to move ahead in the face of pain and adversity.

## SELECTED DISCOGRAPHY

### GARY U.S. BONDS

Dedication . . . . . . . . . . . . . . . . . . . . . . . . . . . . . . . . . . . . . . . . . . EMI
"New Orleans" (Single) . . . . . . . . . . . . . . . . . . . . . . . . Le Grand
On the Line . . . . . . . . . . . . . . . . . . . . . . . . . . . . . . . . . . . . . . . EMI
"A Quarter to Three" (Single). . . . . . . . . . . . . . . . . . . Le Grand
"School Is Out" (Single) . . . . . . . . . . . . . . . . . . . . . . . . Le Grand
"Twist, Twist, Señora" (Single). . . . . . . . . . . . . . . . . . Le Grand

### BRUCE SPRINGSTEEN

Born in the USA . . . . . . . . . . . . . . . . . . . . . . . . . . . . . . . . . . CBS
Born to Run. . . . . . . . . . . . . . . . . . . . . . . . . . . . . . . . . . . . . . . CBS
Darkness on the Edge of Town . . . . . . . . . . . . . . . . . . . . . CBS
Greetings From Asbury Park N.J. . . . . . . . . . . . . . . . . . . . . CBS
Nebraska. . . . . . . . . . . . . . . . . . . . . . . . . . . . . . . . . . . . . . . . . CBS
The River . . . . . . . . . . . . . . . . . . . . . . . . . . . . . . . . . . . . . . . . . CBS
The Wild, the Innocent & the E Street Shuffle. . . . . . . . . . CBS

Cook, Bruce. *Listen to The Blues.* New York: Charles Scribner's Sons, 1973.

Ferris, William. *Blues from The Delta.* New York: Anchor Books, 1979.

Gillet, Charlie. *The Sound of the City.* New York: Outerbridge and Dientsfrey, 1970.

Goldman, Albert. *Elvis.* New York: McGraw-Hill Co., 1982.

Hounsome, Terry and Chambre, Tim. *Rock Record.* New York: Facts on File, 1981.

Marcus, Greil. *Mystery Train.* New York: E. P. Dutton, 1976.

Palmer, Robert. *The Deep Blues.* New York: The Viking Press, 1981.

Palmer, Tony. *All You Need Is Love.* New York: Grossman Publishers Division of Viking Press, 1976.

Roberts, John Storm. *Black Music of Two Worlds.* New York: Morrow, 1974.

Miller, Jim, ed. *The Rolling Stone Illustrated History of Rock and Roll.* New York: Random House Books. Rolling Stone Press, 1976.

*The Rolling Stone Interviews* Volume I, edited by the editors of *Rolling Stone.* New York: Warner Paperback Library, 1971.

Torres, Ben Fong, ed. *The Rolling Stone Rock 'n' Roll Reader.* New York: Bantam Books, 1974.

Shaw, Arnold. *Honkers and Shouters.* New York: Macmillan, 1978.

————. *The World of Soul.* New Jersey: Cowles Book Company, 1970.

Whitburn, Joel. *Record Research,* based on *Billboard* Magazine, 1949–1971.

# INDEX

## ABOUT THE AUTHOR

Gene Busnar is a songwriter, musician, and author of the following books on popular music: *It's Rock 'N' Roll, Superstars of Rock, Superstars of Country Music,* and *Superstars of Rock 2.*